Through a Glass Darkly

To Michael —

With love & thanks.

By

Christine

Christine M. Stearns

2016

A Brief Introduction…

In this slim little volume are some of my favorite
poems that I have written over the years. I believe
that poets see through the veil every now and then,
and my poetry usually comes from one of those
experiences. Those small epiphanies that happen
every day, even when you least expect it.

When I have one of those epiphanies, I try to get it
on paper. And sometimes, it really works, and the
result is magic! I hope that you enjoy these
glimpses, and that one or two of them speak to your
soul.

Like St. Paul says, right now we see imperfectly.
We see only "through a glass darkly." Some day
we will see so much better, but not yet. Not yet.

The book closes with an essay entitled "Through a
Glass Darkly." The essay builds on several
reflections on some of the great literature we have
read together, showing how each one of those
pieces can give us some light on the journey.

Thank you, from the bottom of my heart, for taking
the time to think about the journey with me.

After all, the unexamined life is not worth living.
Remember?

Acknowledgements

I want to thank my husband, the love of my life. Without him, none of this would be possible. I want to thank my sons and daughters--they have given me wings and taught me that love grows and grows. The more we give away, the more it comes back to us.

I want to thank my mom and dad—my first and best teachers about all the things that matter. I also want to thank my brothers and sisters and my extended family. I am lucky enough to have grown up surrounded by love.

I want to thank my colleagues and friends at St. Thomas Aquinas High School, and my students— who have taught me so much about courage and perseverance.

I want to thank my dear friend, Father Tony Mulderry—who taught me that the challenge of being a good mom, grandma, daughter, sister, friend, and teacher is "authentic, genuine, and holy."

Finally, I want to thank all the teachers I had throughout my school and university career. You have shown me the way, and I bow gratefully to you.

And, underneath all of this, I thank God for my faith. O Lord, I believe. Help my unbelief. What a perfect prayer. Amen.

Autumnal Rain

The rain is gray and noiseless.
It settles on my hair,
Pressing it wetly, close to my head.

The sky is so full of clouds
That it seems empty.
A slate with nothing written on it.

The sun simply forgot today.
It just never rose.
I struggled through the day.

The grayness and cold got in my bones.
And you.

You're not coming home for dinner.
I feel so alone.

Baby Sleeping

Such tiny breaths.
So little.
I watch and hold my breath,
In awe.
This little life—
So perfect.
What will she become?
I treasure each tiny toe,
And stand speechless by her crib.
I count her fingers,
And watch the rise and fall
Of her little chest.
I wait anxiously for her to awaken.
I want to hold her in my arms.
And sing to her softly.
I cannot even believe
That she is here,
In this world, and
That she is mine.
I treasure the flutter of her eyelids,
The softness of her cheeks, the
Wholeness of her life,
And her mystery.
A gift beyond all speaking.
I am hushed, and
Reverent.

Back to Heaven

I run back to heaven in my dreams.
There was a time, there was a place...
Sometimes when I awaken, I can still hear
Echoes of it, whispering secrets that are
Just beyond my reach.
Just beyond the reach of words,
Maybe the music of the spheres.
Sometimes I hear the music in the morning.
In the quiet of the morning, before the day begins.
And this morning, when I walked along the beach,
The dawn hung low, just below the horizon.
Not yet light, and yet, in the distance,
A bank of clouds were lit up from below.
It looked like a faraway city in the sky,
A place where angels were awakening,
Drinking coffee and eating croissants.
Getting ready, as they must,
To begin their days too, and walk beside us.
I felt a sudden coolness.
The brush of wings?
Suddenly, the sun broke the horizon,
Splashing blood red on the ocean,
Like a heart.

Call to Adventure

Come, my dear friend.
You've hesitated long enough.
I have told you what I know, so now you must
depart.

I do not know where the winds will carry you.
But I know that you will be wonderful.
I have taught you how to swim in deep water.
So swim.

I have held your hand for a long time now, and
It has been my honor to do so.
But, now I need to let you go and find out for
yourself.
And you are ready for the great adventure.
More than ready.

Keep your balance now, and
Keep to the middle path. Nothing too much, you
remember.
Know thyself.
That is your lifelong mission.
Because your self is always in motion, always
changing.
Like the tides.
Like the sky.
Like the endless days and endless nights.
All numbered somewhere.

We have had such a wonderful time together, and
We have made music together.
Music never really disappears, you know.

It hangs up there in the atmosphere.

Waiting for the right moment to slip back inside
your mind.
Like a warm cotton blanket on a chilly night.
Like dark chocolate and deep red wine.
Like a cherry blossom behind you.
Like a red, red rose.
Deep
And
Red
Like blood
Like wine.

Cathedral

I sit in row seven, seat F.
My face pressed against the glass,
As if I could breathe the cold air outside.

Raindrops glisten on the glass,
As we tumble through grey clouds
Spun like whispers against the stormy sky.

The plane drops.
There is that weird tumble inside me.
The shock of anti-gravity felt momentarily.
Somewhere in the back of the plane, a baby cries.
I imagine his mother patting his back, reassuring
him.
All will be well, all will be well.

I feel the silence all around me.
Hundreds of people breathing as one,
Willing the pilot to land the big ship.

The lightning crashes around us,
Casting a shimmering blaze on the ocean below.
Along the shoreline, the big condominiums huddle
together,
Their shoulders hunched against the wind and the
storm.

I feel very close to you.
I feel strangely unafraid.
The plane is as quiet as a cathedral,
And I can almost feel the prayers being lifted up.
Can they buoy the big airship up? I think maybe
they can.

The Lord is my shepherd.
I shall not want. He maketh me to lie down
In green pastures…my cup runneth over.
The cabin is hushed with silent prayers. A modern
cathedral.
For thine is the power and glory.

The wheels bump the pavement, and the plane skids
Sideways…the earth has grabbed her and pulled her
down.
Down to the earth safely again. People start
laughing
And turn on their cell phones. Seatbelts unbuckle…
But there was a moment,
When it all stood still. And I remember it,
My face against the glass, feeling you slip away.
Not yet.
Amen.

Chance Encounter

January. Fort Lauderdale Beach.
Warm and sunny,
But with a nip in the air.

I go for a swim, and run for my towel
Grateful for its warmth against
The wind.

I go up to the fountain to rinse my feet.
There's a young mother there, with
Two little ones. She is drying her daughter, and
Her son stands off to the side,
Shivering.
Eyes wide with cold.

I offer my towel,
Holding it open.
He dives into it, and I
Wrap him right up.
"Merci, madame," he says.
"Merci."

I tell her to keep it,
And she smiles.

As I walk away, all I can see is
His little face, and big brown eyes,
Swathed in the towel.
He smiles once again.
And blinks.

Merci.

Christmas Dreams

I remember, sitting on the couch,
My nose pressed up against the glass,
Hoping for snow.
Searching the dark sky for a sleigh.
And I remember…
Sitting underneath the tree,
Hypnotized by the twinkle lights,
Dreaming, hoping.
I remember the frenzy of presents,
Mom and Dad bewildered by the chaos
Of children they had made.
Those days are gone, but they linger in my
memories.
Like fragrant prayers.
Now, I am the Mom, making lists and trying,
Oh so hard, to make all the Christmas dreams come
true
Of those entrusted to me.
And it occurs to me—that is what Christmas is
about.
Trust.
Thank you, Lord, for trusting me to do my best.
Thank you, Lord, for walking on this earth,
somewhere
Long ago, and breathing like we breathe.
Somewhere in the dark tonight, a rush of wind.
Angels carrying your message still into the crush of
modern nights.
You love us still…you love us still.
You wait patiently for us to call, and look for you.
A rush of wings.
Our wings fluttering still.
And we are still
Hoping.

Christmas Prayer

In the quiet of the night, I sit alone in the dark by
the tree and listen to the darkness.
I know that sometimes, Lord, you whisper. The
lights whisper on the tree.
Help me to listen to the whispers, and hear, once
again,
The promise of Christmas.

Tonight when the night wind blows the stars across
the sky,
Let me imagine the star that guided the kings of old
to your stable.
To kneel at your cradle, to worship you with quiet
hearts.
Help me to open my soul to your gentle wisdom.
And to be, once again, like a child.

When the world presses in too closely,
Let me remember to think of my blessings.
Let me try to imagine a baby, born in a stable,
shivering.
His lovely mother shivering with awe.
And the whole world shivering with his quiet
majesty,
Angels we have heard on high, sweetly singing o'er
the plain.
Their song echoing from the distant mountains,
As heaven touches earth, once again.

God become Man. Understated majesty.
Born to us again in our hearts and in our minds.
Come to us, Lord.
Come to us, Lord.

We wait quietly in the darkness tonight,
Hoping to hear the whisper
Of your promise,
Once again.

Ah.

Dancing. Still Dancing

I love to dance.
My friends all laugh at me.
They think that, maybe, I'm too old for that.
Hip grinding, foot stomping, eyes closed in rapture.
Sweat.
Letting the music…words and music…that is,
Carry me away, back to younger days.

Carried on the notes, lifted on the words,
I am lighter, I am freer, I am young.

What a foolish illusion, they caution.
Time passes, and we are what we are.
Ah, yes. And yet.
If it is foolish, let it be.
I have been a fool for lesser things,
And will again,
Hopefully.

I will keep dancing, each step a small defiance
Of the gravity of years, and time,
And death.
Sweating joyfully, till my feet ache.

Like Sisyphus, pushing the rock up the hill
To a rock and roll rhythm, and a
Back beat,
Thumping like a hammer
In the back of his brain, in
The depths of his soul.

Dreamscape for my Birthday Morning

Just before dawn, I lay almost awake,
Tangled in my sheets and in memories of you.

The faintest smell, as of roses,
Hovered just beyond my reach,
And morning coffee, and
Laughter
Echoed in my heart.
And it was you.

I felt it slipping, and desperate
To hold on, I must have pulled the
Sheet over my head, as if that could
Keep you closer,
Closer.

We are as we were…me a young mom,
Slipping away for a morning coffee,
With my Mom.
Stolen minutes and quiet laughter.
If only I had known.

We were in a green garden,
Butterflies and robins flutter nearby,
And the sunlight dapples the deck.
We pull our chairs close, and whisper,
As if fearful that loud voices will
Shatter the moment.

Your green eyes laughing.
My green eyes answering.
How long has it been since we sat like this?
How delicious the coffee,
How warm your voice.

I kiss you goodbye.
You wave to me and smile,
And I move the sheet
And wake up.
And you are gone again.

Flying

Flying north to Michigan,
37,000 feet above the earth…
the landscape stretches out beneath me—
a brown quilt in November.

It's been ten years since my mother died.
I search for her everywhere.

Below me, I see a highway
Cutting through the mountains.
We drove that road together—
So many times.

She is not there.

I close my eyes
And listen to the engines hum and roar…

I must have dozed.
Slowly, I open my eyes,
Surprised at having slept.

We have risen, and the landscape
Below has changed.
Now the earth is covered with a
Blanket of clouds.

It looks like snow.
I can no longer see the earth.
I feel weightless, suspended between two worlds.
The sky around me is a heartbreaking blue—
Like a Madonna cloak in an old painting.

The morning sun lights up the clouds from the east.

And then suddenly I notice
An improbable full moon hung up in the blue

And I hear a whisper of her voice
Holding me close once more.

For Benjamin

Deep. Winter.
Deep blue winter cold.
Ice in the wind tonight.
A night so cold it hurts to breathe.
Deep in December.

The snow is swirling outside my window.
My body struggles to bring him forth.
I sweat with the fury of it all.
I am burning with fire and fighting for life.

And in his own time,
He arrives in the world.
Red faced and frightened.
I hold him close and his heart
Beats with mine.

He is warm next to me and we
Hold close to each other.
His blue eyes open and look into mine.
Welcome to the world, my little one.

I will protect you from every harm.
I will be your guardian angel.
I feel my body adjust to new rhythms,
The rhythm of his breathing becomes my own.

Deep in December,
We protect each other.
All night long I hold him and
Look at him.
With adoration.
And I bless him.

He is mine.
Mine.

For James

He came quietly into the world.
Long ago.
Years ago.
And took his place among the warriors
On the quest.

He conducted himself with dignity.
And honor.
Quietly.
Hearty laughter, eager to lend a hand.
When he spoke with you,
He looked you in the eye, and
You felt the weight of his attention.

And he has slipped away.
Quietly, once again.
And attention must be paid.

We sat at his side,
Ushering him safely from this world to the next.
Watching as he merged
The two worlds.
Quietly.

The morning came and went.
The birds of summer whistled their songs.
And he went with them.
Carried on a summer breeze,
Flying softly as the wind lifted his spirit.

And he is young and strong again.
Getting comfortable with strength returned.
Smiling his soft smile.
Eager to lend a hand.

A gentle man.
A man.

For Jessica

I will never get over what has happened to me.
I will never see the world in the same way again.
I can hardly breathe.
I can hardly believe.

She sleeps in my arms.
So tiny. So sweet.
My daughter myself.
Our lives now woven together in a mystery
Too majestic for words.

She is so fragile.
But she has a lusty cry.
And when she looks in my eyes,
I melt inside.

Her daddy holds her in his arms
And I know that he
Would do anything for her.
Anything at all.
We have both begun to learn about love
In an entirely different way.

At night, we lie down in our bed,
With her resting between us.
Filled with wonder and awe,
We hold hands gently
Around this miracle of love,
This miracle of love.

For Mom

We strolled, side by side,
down the beach,
picking up shells,
scattered by the careless ocean,
jewels beneath our feet.

We talked, side by side,
and laughed, as we walked along,
the sun on our shoulders,
the wind kissing our sun burned cheeks.
The children scampered nearby,
caught up in the magic of the morning,
jewels beneath our feet.

We talked of everything,
and nothing. We used to say
that we were solving
the problems of the world,
laughing, knowing, no one
ever really does that.

When vacation days were done,
we carefully packed up the shells,
and brought them home,
half hoping that we could pack up
the magic of morning in the little
jewels, and bring that magic home with us.
It never really worked.

Now, I still have the shells.
Sitting in my bathroom in a jar.
And, oh, how I wish I could walk with you today.
Down that sun drenched beach,
and laugh and talk of nothing.

The children have all grown,
as children will.

I miss you so.
Walk with me today.
Sit on my shoulder and
whisper to me.
I love you.

For Nicholas

I love to watch you running in the sun.
Your smile lights up even the darkest day.
You are so young, and strong.
Like a puppy loping in the spring.
Dancing in and out of flowers,
Following a good smell in the woods.

You have the brownest eyes,
That shine like the polished stones
That rest at the bottom of a crystal clear
River, rushing by in the spring sunshine.
You sparkle like the sun,
Dappling the ocean on a
Saturday morning, while in the distance,
Sailboats carve white slices in the blue.

You smile, and my heart soars,
Caught up in the wind,
Sailing out over the water,
And into the far horizon
Of light.

Jasmine on the wind,
Light as a whisper,
My soul lifts on the
Wings of your smile.

Graduation Night

I sit in the dark on the stage,
And watch them walk by in their gowns.
They try not to stumble as they cross the stage,
Their names announced to the world.
Their mamas and papas so proud tonight.
But—I remember them in their uniforms,
Sitting in rows and raising their hands.
I remember the countless essays they wrote,
Pouring out their thoughts about what we had read.
And my eyes blur with tears for a minute.
What an honor it's been to teach them.
As they walk by the stage, their voices echo
In my mind, in my mind, in my mind.
I hear Hamlet, Ophelia, and Lear.
I hear Othello and Desdemona,
And Iago, always snickering in the corner.
And Cordelia with tears in her eyes.
Her tears like diamonds, of course.
And loyal Kent saying no need to thank him.
And Goneril and Regan sniping.
And Antigone pleading her case, and
Creon too stubborn to listen.
And Stanley threatening Blanche, and
Stella choosing the Streetcar named Desire,
And Jake Barnes learning to drink the wine,
Just for the taste, just for the joy.
And Lady Brett Ashley twinkling her eyes,
And the Count pouring champagne.
And Edna swimming out too far,
Too far to get back as the ocean whispered.
And Robert Lebrun's goodbye because I love you.
And I know that I have loved them too,
And tonight we must say goodbye,
But we know that we will not forget.

I am the teacher of athletes,
You will honor my style when you surpass me.
Long have you timidly waded holding a plank by
the shore.
Now I will you to be a bold swimmer,
To jump into the sea, rise again, nod to me, shout,
and
Laughingly dash with your hair.
But remember, my words itch at your ears till you
understand them.
Sound your barbaric yawp across the rooftops of the
world.
I will be watching with eyes of love
And a grateful heart.

Honk

I hold my air in tight,
And go down deep.
The water's all around me,
In my eyes and in my hair.

It feels cool, and it holds me in.
I stay down and look up at the sky
Through the water.

When I breathe out I make
Big bubbles with edges that
Rise sparkling and
Burst on the surface of the water.

The sky over me looks pale and yellow.
Too far away.
I pretend that I am lost,
Trapped under the ice that isn't really there,
But could be if it were not summer.

Then, with a heroic push,
I punch through the crust of ice and
Whoosh,
I splash free.

I am saved.
I am found and the air is still clear.

The lake laughs and giggles in splashes.
The sun smiles patiently.
The far away goose honks
"how silly"
to me.

Honk.
Honk.

I swim for shore.

I am Like a Song

I am like a song,
Sung far away and softly,
Drifting over treetops like a memory
Somewhere on a summer night.

My melody's suspended,
Hanging just out of reach in mid air,
But only for a moment,
And then it's gone.

You could try to hold me always,
But I'll slip away from you.
Though I will haunt you like a memory,
Like a delicious memory,
Like the cool remembered taste of
Ice cream songs at midnight
And winter fires
That crumble into
Embers
So

Slowly.

I Love the Way You Write…

I love the way you write—and think.
And yet.
Following a thread, as you love to do,
Is a fine amusement for a summer afternoon.
But—please don't badger me with thoughts
About the political scene.
Buried under tests and essays as I am—
The chronic complaint of an English teacher—
I look up, and right now—
I see only paper.
Under the pile of essays, I huddle,
And imagine sky…
And ocean.
And a chilled glass of white wine,
While I watch white sails slip
Over the horizon.
I feel bullied by blogs these days.
I almost don't even want to hear the words
Liberal conservative left right
I am somewhere in the middle,
Thinking of white wine, and horizons,
And sky.

Sunflower

I never saw a sunflower
Looking at its fellow.
Instead their faces turn
Up to the sky.
As if waiting for the sun
To warm their sturdy bodies,
As if waiting for the rain
To slake their thirst.

When in the golden summer
You come upon a field of them,
It is like a congregation
Enthralled, enraptured.
Down every pew
They stand, faces
Lifted to the heavens.
Their seeds like speckled
Eyes, drinking in the sky.

They do not judge each other,
Or use their fellows as a
Mirror. Their thoughts are
Concentrated heavenward.

Perhaps we ought to take a
Lesson from our brothers of the fields,
And lift our faces much more
Often to the sky.

I-75

I grew up in Michigan, and had three sisters there.
And we had a Mom—she taught us everything we needed
To know to become good moms ourselves.
Now, at this moment in my life,
The four of us have scattered,
And mom has left us to find our own way.
We are sprinkled up and down the continent….
Michigan, Tennessee, Georgia, and Florida.
Mystic names with mysterious echoes of our childhood.
Fifteen hundred miles between us,
Great Lakes to the Atlantic coastline.
And I-75 runs down the spine of the eastern seaboard.
I think of us, at this moment,
Connected by an artery or cars and trucks, headlight and taillights—
Carrying our lifeblood and our words…like whispers in a wire.
The cell phones and telephone lines
Carry our thoughts, each into the
Others' hearts…pumping our blood, and
Thoughts, and sisterhood up and down the
I-75 corridor. As I drift into sleep tonight,
A million cars are humming along the conduit of I-75.
They are like my thoughts, running up to you.
And overhead, far away, watching from a star,
Like the moon shimmering on the mountains along I-75…
Mom.

Mermaid

I went swimming naked in the lake
Early this morning.
Before you were awake.
The air hung over the water, still and heavy.
Nothing moved.
Not a breath of wind.
Even the morning doves were still asleep.
The water was flat and warm.
I slipped in and it held me,
Caressed me.
The water rippled over my body and
I felt strong and clean.
I was warm and easy in the lake.
I stretched long and pulled hard.
I was smooth in the water.
I felt, for a moment, as if my body could
Breathe water, or maybe the water was like air.
Liquid air.
Then the term liquid was redefined
In my mind.
It is drinkable silk. It is softness of
Slow kisses. It is warm touches of
Water like air.
I was astonished at the beauty of it all.
Slowly, the sun rose overhead.
I think it smiled down at the girl
All alone in the
Middle of the lake.
Later, when others were beginning to stumble
From their beds, I swam quietly to shore
And wrapped myself in a huge white towel.
I sat on the beach and felt my cheeks flush a secret
pink.
I felt clean and cool.

I felt new.
Let the day begin.

Moon Boy (Benjamin)

I wonder who is up there tonight,
Sitting on the moon.
Is he looking down at me and
Does his momma sing him a song
Before she tucks him into bed?

Where does he sleep at night?
Is it hard to sleep at all
With all the glowing light
That's all around him?

Momma says that men have flown
Up there in rocket ships of steel
And they found only dust and
Air that wasn't even real
Enough to breathe.

No little boys.
No mommas and
No beds.

I've thought about it,
And I don't believe it.
Because, just now,

I saw him wink at me.

Mother Angel

Sometimes, when I least expect it,
My heart wonders about heaven, and
My thoughts turn to you.

The world is too much with us.
I think there must have been a time
Before this incarnation,
When I wandered freely over
The hills of heaven, with angels as
My companions. They knew that I would
Face my test someday…they probably
Worried and wondered, would I be all right.

Would they have to come and lift me up
When I stumbled and lost my way.
And, you have joined them now.
You lift me up when I am troubled.

Someday, I hope to join their legions,
And whisper gentle words to someone
Who has lost her way,
Soft whispers carried on the wind,
Into the heart and into the soul.

Lifting her past the dangers, and
Turning her back to the light.

For Christopher—My Blue Eyed Boy

I gaze into his eyes
And kiss his cheek,
And I am filled with
Wonder.

I quietly count his fingers
And his toes, and
Touch his little chest
With a kind of reverence.

I listen to his heartbeat,
And remember the picture on
The ultrasound—
Four chambers pumping,
Pumping away…
Life.

His hair is white as sunlight
Tiny wisps of it,
Fluffy and soft.

He looks at me with
Eyes that speak of
Unspeakable trust.
And I will never betray it.

Born on the second day of your
Law school journey.
(Will he one day be
an attorney!)
His daddy passed out cigars
To his professors
To announce his son's
Arrival in the world.

And I quietly adored him,
And kissed his eyes.

Nap

The afternoon sunlight
Dapples the room.
Lazy and languid,
I curl up for a moment—
Just for a moment—
To clear my head.

A cotton blanket is just
Out of reach, but I reach for it,
And feel its
Softness surround me.
Just for a moment,
I close my eyes.

I listen to the wind outside,
And the rain patter on the window.
And the day fades away—
Into a hum.
I surrender to sleep.
Sweet surrender.
Sweet silence roars over me,
And I
Accidentally
Sleep.

Night Time

Momma tucks me in cool sheet
And turns on my fan.
Teddy Bear is waiting in bed for me.
He breathes softly.

His little tummy is warm and
Just only moving up and down
So I can see it.

Cool nighttime kisses in the quiet
From Daddy.
He brushes my hair
Back out of my eyes with his hand.

It feels warm and smells soapy.
I feel like I'm slipping down and
Letting go of the day.

Falling.

Far away cars in the distance
On the road
Whisper past.

Far away there is a train.
I hear the whistle in the darkness.
It sounds sad.
But why.

The night swallows their sound and
I
Fall
Down.

November Rain

It has been raining for
Six straight days now
And the rain has started
Leaking into my
Soul.

The sky is gray.
The water's gray.
All color has been stripped
From the landscape
Except brown and
Gray.

I run along the asphalt
Road, polished black and slick
By the cold November rain.
A car passes me and throws
Icy slush all over me.
The wind tears at my jacket
And my scarf,
Tearing my eyes.

I feel an emptiness in my
Soul
That frightens me.

Luckily, I am soon home,
Surrounded by the noise of children.
The clamor scares away the shadows
That had dogged me on the road.

Once more, I have kept the dark at bay.
But it is out there, whispering
Of the coming bleak cold of the winter.

On the Arrival of a New Little One

Coming softly into the world,
Hardly big enough to matter,
Or so it seems to someone
Who knows nothing at all.

Because, you have changed the world.
The world will never be the same
Now that you are here.
You came softly as a whisper,
But your whisper roars in my ears and my heart.

And it says—nothing will ever be the same.
I count your fingers and toes,
I worship your tiny breathing.
I hold you in my arms, so small,
And search your eyes for recognition.

You have come recently from heaven,
Trailing clouds of glory,
And sometimes, when you look off into the corners
Of the room,
I think you still see angels.

I watch the rise and fall of your tiny chest,
And I believe in miracles.
I am brought to my knees with a
Grateful and humble heart.

You cry in the night, and
My heart leaps up, knowing
Secrets that it has never known
Until now.

I will not let you down.

I will not let you down.
I believe.
I believe.
Amen.

Passing

I see myself…I don't know why exactly…
Swimming into heaven.
The waters through which I swim are clear
And crystal blue, sunlight dappled, and warm.
I swim to a far shore, and I swim well.
The weight of earth falling off me as I move
Through the water.
Standing at the other shore, waiting for me
Is my Mom.
My sweet and beautiful Mom.
The cancer has fallen away.
Her face is young and smiling, her lovely
Hair restored.
She stands, dressed in a white dress, long
And simple, flowing into the water…
Waiting for me.
When I arrive at the far shore,
Naked, dripping wet,
And unashamed,
She welcomes me, arms wide.
I step into her sweet embrace,
Inhale the scent I have missed for so long.
And breathe.
Just breathe.
And I am home.

Pearl Harbor Visitation—the Arizona Memorial

This morning the sun is sparkling on the quiet bay.
The waves lapping at the rocky shore,
The blue surface of the ocean not revealing
Any awareness of what
I know lies beneath its
Translucent skin.
Dappled in sunlight, the surface sparkles
As with a million diamonds,
Or pearls.

Full fathom five thy father lies,
Of his bones are coral made.
Those are pearls that were his eyes,
Nothing of him that doth fade,
But doth suffer a sea change,
Into something rich and strange.
Sea nymphs hourly ring his knell,
Ding dong.

I stare down into the water.
The oil leaks out onto the surface still.
Like tears.
I feel the weight of the loss
Over all the years.
A distant harbor bell tolls out its lonely song.
Ding dong.
I quietly tremble in the sunlight
Like a teardrop afraid to fall.

And then quietly, and quite unexpectedly,
Something catches me unawares,
A sea change.
Into something rich and strange.
A whisper of wind lifts my hair.

A whisper of sunlight and the hum of orchids
And I say a prayer,
Without knowing that I am saying it
(which is always the best kind I think) and
hear a gentle sigh of
wind or water or
sea changes
and pearls in the
harbor.

Rush Hour

Morning.
Rush hour. Red traffic lights dam the flow
Of cars and trucks and busses.
Their engines heaving steam at intersections.
Heaving, hissing, panting, waiting.

I hurriedly flip my vanity mirror down,
Slam on the lipstick I didn't get to use at home.
Windows down, the warm steamy early morning air
Whispering sweaty promises of day.
I glance over at the car next to me.
Another mom, hurriedly putting on lipstick.

We grin at each other.
Sort of.
Click.
Wordless understanding.
She smiles,
A little sadly.
I almost smile back.
The light turns green.

Gone.

Secrets and Promises

The night is finally quiet.
All the kids are tucked away,
And fans are humming in the darkness,
Protecting them against the noises
That might trouble their sleep.
The night engulfs us as
We lay, side by side
In the darkness.
Minds humming.
Drifting and hovering.
Where have you been today?
What did you see?
Did anyone hurt your feelings?
Were you angry or fearful?
Were you bored?

It's good to come home.
We were far away from each other,
But now we are back.
Here is the center of the world, as we know it.
You are my North Star.
I lean toward you and
The universe tips.

Stars lean into the night,
Tilting into the velvet deep.
The rustle of sheets, the
Flutter of covers.

Your breath tickles my neck.
We whisper
Secrets and
Promises.

The Fawn

Seeking patience and wisdom,
I knelt on my mother's grave.
Planting impatiens in July.
An unlikely time for it.

The sun beat down on my back,
And sweat poured from my forehead.
Running like rivers with my tears
Raining down in the soil.

The earth was summer hard.
I brought bottled water and poured it into the mouth
Of the grave. The dirt guzzled it up.
And I cried.

Nestling the pale pink blossoms into the mud
Of tears and sweat and warm bottled water,
My hands worked the earth and wiped my sweaty
face, now
Streaked with mud.

I thought I heard her whisper.
These are not good planting conditions, my darling.
I know, I whispered back.
But still.

I gentled the earth up to the blossoms,
Fluffed them up, and poured the rest of the water
onto their faces.
My tears slowed, and I stood up…
My head spinning in the sun and the heat.

I gathered my tools, stepped back and

Looked at the blossoms, nodding in the gentle breeze,
Shimmering in the sun, like a pink necklace
On her grave.

I went over to my car, parked in the shade,
Thankfully, and tried to gather myself, and find that patience and
Understanding I so dearly sought. I rolled down the windows, and
Closed my eyes, waiting.

Suddenly, a sound in the forest beside me.
I turned to see a lovely young fawn,
Staring in the car window right at me.
I could barely breathe.
Could it be..........

Sestina

The ocean is cold and deep,
With hidden treasures of old.
It keeps itself a mystery
And softly kisses the shore.
I hear the whispers myself,
But I am afraid to know.

For who can ever know
The stories from the deep.
I stand on the shore myself,
And wonder of those from of old,
Who could not reach the shore,
And became a part of the mystery.

For the ocean is always a mystery,
Some power we cannot know.
We stand timidly on the shore,
Afraid to know the deep.
For it is very old,
And I know that myself.

I feel very small myself,
When confronted with its mystery.
It is unchanging and old,
And impossible to know.
Always it beckons to the deep,
But I swim near the shore.

And I cling closely to the shore,
And I am careful with myself.
I am aware of the deep.
I am in awe of the mystery.
And I believe that I know
Some of the secrets from of old.

For I have listened to the old
Secret whispers on the shore.
And I know it is hard to know
The truths about myself.
But I accept the mystery
Of change and life and deep.
For the journey is old and deep,
And the mystery is far from the shore,
As I myself and the ocean both know.

Spring Break in Florida--Aftermath

Haunted by the memories
Of the beach,
I struggle on.
The days are longer now.
Still, I miss the sun wind ocean blue…
I stare out at my students' faces.
I don't remember their names.
I perform for them,
Reaching deep within to do
Hamlet's bedroom scene or
Robert Frost's neat blank verse
Or Tennyson's painfully honest Ulysses,
Or cummings' Buffalo Bill,
But my thoughts tumble freeform
Like seashells scattered
By a careless high tide on
The shoreline mud.
Suddenly, I see the turquoise ocean
Glisten in the image painted in the
Back of my mind.
I struggle on with heavy feet while
Pelicans soar against the blackboard,
Secretly mocking me,
And I miss the wings
I had down there.

Stumbling Home

The baby turtle emerges,
Almost by accident,
On a sunny, windswept beach
At morning.

Confused, he stumbles awkwardly,
The footsteps in the beach are hills
That he must climb.
He tumbles, goes the wrong way—then he
Seems to get his bearings, and
Resolutely starts out for the ocean.

Stunned and excited, a crowd gathers to
Witness his journey. His guardian angels?
Hushed and humbled by the enormity of
His struggle, they hold each other back from him,
Trying hard not to distract him from his quest.

A hundred yards away, the ocean sparkles in the
Early morning sunlight. It looks like a hundred
miles.
Too far.
He struggles bravely on.
It takes forever.
Some people give up and wander off, but most of
them
Stay, determined to see him get to the ocean.

Finally, he seems to smell the water.
He gets surer of himself, of his goal.
He struggles on, little feet like flippers grabbing the
sand
And pulling him forward. He is too little.

When he gets to the water, the waves wash him up
on the shore.
He gains little ground. The whole journey seems
doomed to failure.

The people watch, almost reverent,
Pulling for the little guy—urging him forward with
their thoughts.
But they do not touch.
He attacks the water again. And again. And again.
Finally, he disappears.

There is applause up and down the beach.
I find myself thinking—I bet that
There is applause in heaven
When we turtles stumble home.

Summer Solstice Sunrise #2

I saw a sunrise this morning
As I walked along the beach.
I started my walk in the darkness,
Echoing prayers and starlight
In my mind.

I kept my heart on the horizon,
Waiting for glimpse of the morn.
It seemed as though it would not come
In time for me to see it.
I surrendered to time,
As we must, as we must,
And walked along.

Little did I know
That the daylight was waiting,
Just beyond the reach of my vision.
Waiting for me to stop watching,
Lost in my prayers and my memories,
I must have shuffled along.

When I looked up once again,
My heart leapt up to see that it had all happened
While I was not looking.

I saw a sunrise this morning
That I almost didn't see.
I thought to myself, this one
Would have challenged Monet.
He would have surrendered, thinking,
I cannot do it justice.

Palest pinks and earliest blues
Layered themselves on the horizon.

Heaven?
I am a witness to magic, to the music
Of the heavenly distances.
On the verge of my vision, a spark, and
The sun peeks over the edge of the ocean
And the world bows down, and
I bow down and hold my breath
For a moment
Of time.

The Sky Tonight

The sky tonight overwhelms me.
It stretches endlessly.
Do you understand that?
It is blue still, though growing
Dark around the edges,
Deepening into purples.
The sun is down for the day, yet streams or
Fingers of light stretch up from
Beyond the rim of the earth.
It must still be daylight in
California now, or somewhere,
But here, it's becoming another
Summer night.

When summer's here, it feels
Like it will never end.
Just like the sky that never ends.
It goes on past this valley,
Over the distant trees,
Around the curve of the earth,
And on and on and on.

I drive quietly at the edge of the night
And drink in the darkness.
My car feels at home on the road.
I hear the tires making contact with the pavement,
But I seem to be floating along.
Tonight the long empty highway,
Bathed now in moonlight,
Seems like someone
I'd like to know better.

Three a.m. Feeding

Madonna?
Mama. Mother and child.
Me? Mary? Quiet. Dark.
Drink it in.
His silken cheek soft and full.
Tiny bird mouth sucking, pulling
Life in by mouthfuls.
Tender sleep, eyes watching me even
In his sleep.
Sweet dreams come and go so quickly.
What does he see?

Fields of sheep, wooly white against the green?
Angel wings, pink and pale blue fluttering?
Trailing clouds of glory still?

He might see that.
And I see him, all white and softness,
Holding daylight down to earth.
Or heavenly light down to earth.

What do you see, your eyes flickering?
Me?
Your daddy?

He won't tell me.
But he whispers, sleeps, and sighs.
He sinks deeper into me.
Becoming a part of me.
I breathe with him and
Slip into sleep.

I sleep into the morning still sitting up and
Holding him.

And then I wake, finding my nighttime
Vigil suddenly
Over.
Six a.m.
How?

To My Sister

When we were little,
I was always watching out for you.
And I remember the day
You learned to say my name—
Sort of.

I remember blanket tents,
Held up with tables and chairs.
How precisely you would
Arrange the pillows.
How you loved to pretend that you
Were asleep.
How you sucked your two fingers.
(I never saw anyone else do it that way.)

I remember new Easter dresses, and
Barbie dolls under the old oak tree.
You wobbling on your two wheeler,
Crying for your training wheels,
Me running after you,
Shouting encouragement.

I remember roller skates on the sidewalk.
The old kind with the key.
I tightened your skates for your little foot.
But they hurt you.

I remember taking you to the park,
And pushing you too high.
Walking to school…with heavy feet and
Heavy hearts. Hurrying home to
Cartoons and snack.
A million memories.
And always you…

My little sister.

Funny, how we have children of our own now.
And they have grown.
And now they have their own little ones.
How did the years slide by like that?
I sit with my granddaughter on my knee,
And feed her snacks and watch cartoons,
And remember you.
And me.

Tribute

We were the luckiest kids in the world.
Surrounded by love.
Surrounded by love.
And she was the center, the heart of it all.
We circled around her, like small satellites.
We were stronger because of her love.

And we feel her absence, and we miss the sound
Of her voice, of her laughter.
And yet.
Sometimes in the night she still whispers to us.
When the noise of the day subsides.
So we listen and wait. We listen and wait.
For the whisper will come in our dreams in the
night.

For love like that, such mighty love, goes on and
on.
And now.
We are the centers of our own circles of children.
We are her mighty love in their lives.
And we whisper our prayers for them in the night.
And she listens and knows.
And the love, mighty love,
Goes on.

Valkyrie

I hover, breathlessly—
Poised over the battlefield.
I smell the blood rising like a red mist.
My wings aflutter,
My heart aflutter too.

Below me, the battle rages.
Men fighting for their mortal lives,
Crying out with their last breath,
Eyes wide with fear.
They call for their mothers.
Do they see me watching them?

I watch the tide of the battle turn.
As if pulled by the secret moon.
I watch for the cowards,
And when I see them, slinking
Away from the moment of honor,
I send a thunderbolt,
Right into their hearts.

The brave man I will reward
Either with victory or with death.
But if he dies,
He will sleep with me tonight,
In Valhalla.
And glory will forevermore
Be his.
Be brave, my warrior prince.
I am watching.

Hovering on the wind
Carried over the plain,
Ready to ride the updraft.

Winter Morning Run

I feel the grayness of the morning in me.
I press against the cold.
The road is hard, frozen.
It is deep winter and too cold for a morning run.

In spite of that, the dawn is persistently unfolding.
Or so it seems.
Above the frozen lake, not sun yet.
But a thinness, a lightness in the sky
That suggests that it is coming,
Eventually.

The distant forest is rimmed
Above with pink.
I run the frozen road and listen for the sun.
Nothing moves.

My breath mists in the cold.
I feel the frozen stones beneath my feet,
Angry in the darkness.
Hard-edged and unmovable.

I look up again, and find that
The sunrise must have happened
When I wasn't looking.

Suddenly, the sun is there—
Golden in the pale morning,
Startling the secret birds from frozen branches,
Where they must have been hiding,
Waiting.

A timid warmth begins to creep
Along the landscape—white

With winter snow and
Deep with cold.

Below the crust, do the
Stones feel it.
I run clumsily and
Wonder.

Winter Soup

The wind whips down the street,
Lifting the bottom of my school uniform skirt.
My knees are already red and raw
From fighting the angry wind.

Buried in a scarf that muffles my face,
My eyelashes have glued themselves together,
With my frosty breath.
I lean forward, pushing into the wind,
And it pushes back.

The road is crystallized ice, not
Sparkling, though, because there is no sun.
The sky is gray, the ice is gray.
I trudge along, helpless in the face of it all.
And very small.
January in Michigan.
The endless chain of gray days goes on
And on.

Inside the house, I unwrap.
Scarf, mittens, boots, and coat—
Falling like feathers from a molting bird.
Melting puddles in the hall.
I am carried by the smell of the hot
Soup on the stove.
Warm French bread.
Mom says, "Welcome home,
My dear."
She kisses me hello.
Red cheeks warm.
Eyelashes thaw.

I am rich beyond all measure.

Words to My Unborn Child

You were conceived in the fullness of summer.
One August night, warm and still.
I thought you'd ripen slowly in the autumn,
Sleep deep through the long winter and
Blossom in the spring.

May was your chosen month.
A time for tulips and gentle, warming breezes
And rebirth.

But the promise wasn't kept.
Before the harvest was done,
I lost you.

I remember lying in my bed in the October night,
Quick and cool,
Trying to stop the bleeding,
Trying to stop the dull ooze
As life slipped away.

What are we going to do
With the names we picked out for you?

The empty room?

The crib?

Words to Remember

An unexamined life is not worth living.
Socrates.
He was right, you know.
So, when your mind races ahead of you with
questions deep at night,
Try to smile in your heart and know that all is well.

We are, each of us, in our own little boats, from the
moment of our birth.
Carried along on some vast, primordial sea—a sea
we cannot predict or control.
And yet.
There are moments of contact, of understanding.
And these moments are sacred.
Keep to the middle path. Allow moments when you
go a little too far,
But come back to the middle soon. Soon.

We all have obligations, from the moment we are
born.
That's what keeps us human.
Honor the ties that bind you to others.

You must get to know the values. You must figure
out what you stand for.
And then eat your bread and drink your wine with a
merry heart,
For God has already approved that you do so.
Sacred hurts will come.
No one escapes unhurt.
Hold on.
Make it through the night.
Things will look better one morning.
In the meantime, just keep swimming.

Open your eyes in the deep water.
Hold your dive strong and straight.
Roll over on your back when the water is sun
dappled and shallow.
The next wave is coming.

But know that there is a divinity that shapes our
ends.
A benevolent providence at work.
Quietly pulling us toward joy.

So, do the best you can. Brighten your little corner
of the world.
In spite of your doubts and questions,
Keep going.

All love is worthy.
So, wait for it. And trust. It will come like a
whisper on the wind,
When you least expect it. Like faraway music on
the wind.
Watch and see.

Through a Glass Darkly

If I speak in the tongues of men and of angels,

But have not love,

I am a noisy gong or a clanging cymbal.

And if I have the prophetic powers,

And understand all the mysteries and all the

knowledge,

And if I have all faith,

So as to remove mountains,

But have not love,

I am nothing.

If I give away all I have,

And if I deliver my body to be burned,

But have not love,

I gain nothing.

Love is patient and kind;

Love is not jealous or boastful;

It is not arrogant or rude.

Love does not insist on its own way.

It is not irritable or resentful.

It does not rejoice at wrong,

But rejoices in the right.

Love bears all things, believes all things,

Hopes all things, endures all things.

Love never ends.

As for prophecies, they will pass away.

As for knowledge, it will pass away.

For our knowledge is imperfect and our prophecy is

imperfect.

But when the perfect comes, the imperfect will pass

away.

When I was a child, I spoke like a child.

I thought like a child, I reasoned like a child.

When I became a man, I gave up childish ways.

For now we see

Through a glass darkly.

72

But then we will see face to face.

Now I know in part; then I shall understand fully.

Even as I have been fully understood.

So, faith, hope, and love abide, these three.

But the greatest of these is love.

St. Paul's First letter to the Corinthians—Chapter

13, verses 1-13

Written approximately 52 A. D. to the people of the

church in Corinth

This passage, when considered alone, is

spiritually significant and very moving. It may be

the best definition of love that has ever been

written, if such a thing as love can ever be defined.

Paul is discussing the three most important spiritual

gifts here. The greatest gift of the Spirit is not hope

or even faith, but love. This love is not love in an ordinary or general sense of our everyday world, but the very love our heavenly Father poured out for us. We notice that Paul begins by saying that sometimes, people can do very impressive things, seeming to be exceptionally gifted. However, if they do not have love as the primary motivation for what they do, their performances are just that— empty noises, like gongs and cymbals crashing. Human knowledge is always flawed and incomplete. This is apparently as true in his time as it is in ours. Right now, our vision is also incomplete. We see glimpses of heaven, as if through a glass darkly. But in time, in our heavenly Father's time, we will see more clearly, and understand more fully. We will ascend from this incomplete and imperfect incarnation and be like angels. And the way this will be accomplished is through love.

What on earth does all of this mean? Can it be that simple? And that complicated? What should be our goal for our time here on earth? Why do bad things happen to good people? Where does it all end? And how does love figure into the whole experience? How can love be even more important than faith?

A Place to Start—Introductory Thoughts and a Glimpse of Plato and his Cave

These are very difficult questions, and men and women have been trying to answer them for a very long time. Clearly, from the beginning of recorded history, men and women have been trying to understand what this life is all about. From the very first moment that someone could articulate the idea of his or her existence, we have been trying to figure out how we got here, and why we are here. Throughout the ages, the greatest literature has addressed these questions in an infinite number of ways, some more successful than others. Literary scholars talk about three primordial or ontological questions that have been the foundation of all great literature. They can be succinctly stated in the following way: Who am I? Why am I here? Is my life directed by free will or fate?

One of the first secular attempts to answer these questions came from the ancient Greek philosopher we call Plato. His real name is Aristocles and he lived from approximately 427-347 B. C. He was born in Greece, and for a while he wanted to be a politician. However, several things happened that changed his mind and pointed him in a new direction. He saw that many politicians of his time were cruel and dishonest. He saw them sentence his great friend and mentor, Socrates, to death. Eventually, Plato left both Athens and an active political life to travel widely in the ancient world. In 387, he returned to Athens and founded The Academy, a school of science and philosophy that lasted for almost a thousand years. In fact, it could be said to be the first university ever created,

and so, in that sense, it endures even today. In fact,
it has flourished. In order to honor him, his students
gave him the nickname of Plato, a name that means,
"broad shouldered."

Aside from the Old Testament philosophers,
Plato is our earliest recorded great thinker. He
believed that our physical senses are unreliable for
understanding the truth about eternity, but he
believed that such an eternity existed, and he would
call that Truth, with a capital T. We cannot
perceive this Truth with our limited human senses,
although we can come closer to it if we have been
trained. Even so, we see only glimpses of the
Truth. In other words, we see, as men and women,
only "through a glass darkly." He theorized that the
ideal realm exists, and that it is perceived by all
humans before birth. As we live and grow, we
forget this ideal realm, but a vague memory of it

keeps alive our search for spiritual renewal. And at some visceral level, we know that there is much more than this life.

Plato's favorite literary form is called the "dialogue." It is really an essay disguised as a conversation. One person asks questions and actively listens while the other person teaches. Plato honors his friend Socrates by making him be the teaching voice in his dialogues. Perhaps the most famous of all of these dialogues is the one entitled "The Allegory of the Cave." Almost every undergraduate runs into this famous essay/dialogue in the course of his or her study. In spite of the fact that this piece of literature has been around for over 2400 years, scholars still engage in an active debate about what Plato was trying to say in it.

Supposedly, the purpose of this dialogue is to discuss the idea of who is most qualified to lead the state. However, the essay addresses many more ideas than that, and many readers have found that it speaks very powerfully to them about a number of issues, including the process of growing up and leaving "home," and about duty and ethics as well.

An allegory is really an extended metaphor, and that is what this essay presents us with. The teacher tells his student that he is going to offer him an allegory that will help him to understand the purpose in life. He says that we should picture the human condition in the following way: We are all prisoners in an underground cave, bound to each other in some fashion, facing the rear wall of the cave. We cannot turn around to see the mouth of the cave, but it is pretty clear that there is a great light out there somewhere, casting shadows on the rear wall, and these shadows are all we can see. We suspect that there is more going on, but the shadowy reflections are "real" to us, because at this moment, that is all our senses can perceive.

However, one day, an "instructor" comes down into the cave and unshackles one of the prisoners, forcibly dragging him or her up to the light. In the process of this journey upwards, the prisoner undergoes pain and confusion: "When he is reluctantly dragged up a steep and rugged ascent, and held fast until he is forced into the presence of the sun himself, is he not likely to be pained and irritated…He will require time to grow accustomed to the sight of the upper world. And first he will see the shadows best, next the reflections of men and other objects in the water, and then the objects themselves…last of all he will be able to see the sun". When he can finally see the Sun (or the Truth, or Beauty, or God, or the Good) he will think back on his ignorance when he was in the cave, and

81

he will feel pity for those he left behind. However, he will not feel so much pity that he will want to go back to that life of ignorance and darkness. Having been in the "realms of gold and light," he has no desire to return to the cave. But he must.

Here's the crux of the matter. He must return. When he has had enough time up in the realms of gold and light, and that "enough" is different for every person, he must return to the cave. There, the real work of his life will begin. We do not know the criteria by which "enough" is determined. Plato makes no attempt to stipulate that. He insists, however, that the "philosopher king" must return to the cave after his earthly education is complete. There, he will serve his fellow prisoners. Now, there is no guarantee that this will go well, or that his "wisdom" will be eagerly or warmly received by the prisoners of the darkness. In fact, the prisoners may mock him and say that he is crazy, and that he doesn't know what he is talking about. But every now and then, someone will listen, and in fact, he may be the "instructor" that unties the bonds on another prisoner and sends him or her on their way up to the realms of gold and light.   And in time, he will move the condition of his fellow human beings closer to the light. This is the purpose for which he has been created. And although he does not want to rule, he must. In fact, according to Plato, "the truth is that the State in which the rulers are most reluctant to govern is always the best and most quietly governed, and the State in which they are most eager, the worst". Now, this is a very controversial statement, and taken to extremes, the logic falls apart. Still, there is some merit to what he says. A philosopher king knows more of the wisdom of the realms of gold and light, and longs to dwell there always. Still, he also acknowledges a duty to his fellow man, and will direct his energies, during his lifetime, to helping to improve the human condition. He does not do this for glory or earthly wealth, because his true treasure is not of this world. All of us can think of examples of someone who was very eager for the mantle of leadership, in fact too eager. We have all seen stories play out where someone wants to use that position of power for personal gain, to the detriment of those who trusted him to lead well and honestly. Maybe there is something to Plato's warning against those who are too eager to rule. Of course, for all practical matters, we understand that someone has to want to accept the responsibility of leadership, so, once again we are reminded not to push the idea too far. Plato adds that we should take good care of our philosopher kings so they do not have to worry about having enough to feed themselves and their families and can concentrate their energies on making this world a better place for everyone.

This famous essay is one of the first secular attempts to answer the three primordial questions— Who am I? Why am I here? Is my life directed by free will or fate? The answer that Plato seems to give is that we are "prisoners" of this earthly incarnation temporarily. There is a better place that exists outside of this earthly realm, and some of us are granted a vision or an experience of what it will be like. It is our duty to use our vision or our understanding, as limited as it is, to serve our fellow man, to live honorably and ethically, and do the best we can while we are here. All in all, this is not a bad set of answers to very difficult questions.

We can think of the idea of the essay in the following way. We are born into a situation, shackled to our family members and friends from the moment of our birth. I do not mean the word "shackled" in any pejorative sense here. Rather, we are linked, but forcibly linked by birth to certain people. As friendships and obligations develop, we acquire more and more links or shackles. Suffice it to say, we are bound to certain other people from the moment of our birth. As children, we are content with this situation because it is all we have ever known. However, one day, some instructor removes our bonds, and we begin our ascent to the realms of gold and light. Maybe that instructor is a teacher, but it could be anyone who shows you where your gift is and sets your soul on fire for the first time. As you ascend, or learn, you struggle. It takes a long time to figure out what your mission is, what your gift is, and what should be the purpose of your life. You fall in love with knowledge, with learning, and you want to just keep going further and further in your study. But you can't. You must go back to the cave.

So, you leave the university, with your earthly "degree" in hand, and go back to the cave to serve your fellow prisoner—as an attorney, teacher, researcher, doctor, nurse, housekeeper, computer technician, dental hygienist, banker, or…anything you can think of where you use your gift. There is a part of you that remembers the glory of your time at the university, where you learned your craft or acquired your earthly wisdom, but eventually you understand that those days are gone, and you must move on. So, you work. And some days, it feels like all your work is for nothing; you are accomplishing nothing. But every now and then, you realize that you have made a difference in someone else's life. And you are doing what you were born to do.

Several years ago, my mom died of cancer, after a long and brave battle. And I have been thinking about heaven ever since. I don't think I ever really thought about it much until Mom died, but now I think about it a lot more often. I am willing to bet that this is a pretty universal experience. Once someone you love very much dies, you wonder where they are. As a Catholic and a Christian, I have been raised to believe in an afterlife—a heaven with our loving heavenly Father. And with the choirs of angels singing His praises. We would like to have a little more information about all of that, but we will all have to wait until our appointed time. And so we wonder, and we think about what it all might mean. The truth is, I think about a lot of things I never thought about before. Until you have lost someone that is at the core of your life, the very fabric of your existence, I don't think it hits you. But after that has happened, and you have suffered that kind of core loss, you will never be the same. You think about things more deeply, even if you can't bring yourself to talk about them. I know I do, and many of my friends who have lost a loved one have expressed the same quiet yearning. So, I decided that it was time to write some of these thoughts down. My mom always told me I was going to be a writer. Instead, I became a teacher. And I love doing that. But lately, she has been whispering more insistently from beyond the invisible veil, so I thought I had better get the ideas down on paper.

I remember this one class I took on learning how to write said that you don't really understand something, or even really know how you feel about it until you try to write it down. If there is any truth to that, then this might be an interesting exercise. So, I will begin, and I invite you to come along on this journey. We are going to consider what we can and cannot know about our place here on earth, our heavenly Father, His divine providence, and how to live in this world while it is our time to do so. If we, in fact, can only see "through a glass darkly," then some of the most famous pieces of literature that attempt to address the three big questions could be considered to be various glasses, or mirrors, through which or in which we might get a glimpse of the Truth.

St. Paul tells us that we cannot know the answers to our burning questions about God and heaven and the afterlife right now. Let us look again at that famous passage that we considered at the opening of this writing: "Our knowledge is imperfect and our prophecy is imperfect; but when the perfect comes, the imperfect will pass away. When I was a child, I spoke like a child, I thought like a child, I reasoned like a child; when I became a man, I gave up childish ways. For now we see through a glass darkly, but then face to face. Now I know in part; then I shall understand fully, even as I have been fully understood"(Corinthians 13: 8-12). We see only glimpses right now, through a glass darkly. We can only understand a little bit about why we are here, but we do get glimpses of understanding every now and then. And sometimes, we hear whispers beyond the veil. We suspect, at some very deep and almost visceral level, as Plato did, that there is much more than this earthly incarnation, that a more profound Truth is waiting for us, perhaps even a lasting realm of gold and light.

This morning, I went for a walk along the beach. It was very overcast, and the storm clouds were low and racy across the horizon. At any moment, it looked as if the skies might open up and just pour. But, there were still some hearty souls at the beach, keeping a wary eye on the clouds, and playing in the surf. And, there was this one little boy, about ten years old, playing in the shallows. It was a yellow flag day, and the surf was really choppy—the kind that smashes you right on the shore and then drags you back out. Mean, nasty surf. Well, this little boy was being hammered, but he was not giving up. The waves kept on crashing right on his head, smashing him on the shore, and then dragging him out for another pounding. I am sure that his bathing suit was full of sand and shells, but he looked oblivious to the danger. He was just laughing, and getting pounded. His dad was walking back and forth on the shore, letting the little boy play—if you could call it that. Letting his son get smashed by the waves, anyhow. He smiled a kind of rueful smile at me when I walked by, kept a cautious eye on the sky, and watched his son. I had the feeling that he really wanted to say to him, "Son, that's enough." But he didn't. He kept his distance, kept an eye on him, and let him go. Anyhow, it struck me that I was looking at an apt metaphor for our heavenly Father and us. He lets us get smashed by the waves, lets us get hammered by the stuff that happens in life, and watches carefully from a distance. But, just like this dad was ready to wade out into that water and grab his son if he had to, so too our heavenly father. If we let ourselves, we can sense his presence guiding us, holding us in the palm of His hand. Now, I can feel you saying—

Not always! Sometimes children die, and terrible

things happen to good people. You are right, and it

is very difficult to come to terms with this sort of

injustice. However, I would ask you to be patient.

Let's keep talking and thinking about some of the

great pieces of literature, and how they have

addressed this very difficult idea. Let us

accumulate evidence before we render a verdict.

Think of yourself as a judge, hearing conflicting

testimony from a number of unruly witnesses.

Keep an open mind before you render your verdict.

Another Glimpse—Hamlet, Providence, and Free Will

Lots of the things I have learned and come to believe in are things I have discovered in my studies of great literature. That is true for any student of literature, because the great pieces invite us into a discussion about the most profound ideas ever confronted by any sentient human being. Socrates is famously attributed with the brilliant statement that "an unexamined life is not worth living." Most of us would agree with this statement. Well, perhaps the most famous "examination of life" ever portrayed in a single piece of literature comes from William Shakespeare's play entitled *Hamlet*. Almost every good student reads it in high school, but I can almost guarantee that you can read it again and again, and each time, it will speak to you in a different way. It continues to excite debate among thinkers at the university level today. Just look at the number of Master's and Doctoral theses that touch on *Hamlet* in any given year. So, it should not surprise us that we would want to take a look at what this complex play has to say about the three big questions.

In this play, written around the year 1600, the young prince—who is battling with more problems than any man ought to have to face, fights through a very dark hour of the soul and eventually comes to believe in a divine providence. He says, in the closing at of the play, "There's a divinity that shapes our ends, rough hew them how we will." That divinity is our heavenly father. He shapes the course of our lives, guides us to him, in spite of the fact that we have free will. Make no mistake about that—we do have free will. That is what Hamlet means when he says, "rough hew them how we will." We make millions of free will decisions in the course of a lifetime, and of course they impact the shape of our lives. Still—and this is the tricky part—there is a plan. This is what Hamlet refers to as the "divinity." We decide what to do, and our heavenly Father waits for us to come to Him. Waits and watches, just like the dad pacing the shoreline, watching his son in the waves. His amazing and overpowering love is there to rescue us. After all, remember that Jesus said, "Ask, and it shall be given unto you; seek and you shall find." We can make a mistake in our understanding of this statement. We may read it as some promise of instant gratification. Ask, and you shall have it. Immediately. Just the way you envision it. This understanding is a misreading. Our heavenly Father hears our prayers and answers them. However, the answer does not always come in the form we expect it. Let's face it—sometimes our prayers are foolish. Always He is wiser than we are. Can you think of a time when you prayed for something, even prayed fervently for it, and now, from the vantage point of your further years of life, you know it was not a good thing to pray for? I certainly can. I would be embarrassed to tell you some of the things I prayed for once upon a time.

However, our prayers are answered in time, and if we look with the eyes of faith, we will see the truth in this. Time is such a difficult concept. When we are impatient for a problem to be resolved, time seems to move so slowly. When we are experiencing a time of joy and satisfaction, time just seems to fly. When we try to understand the idea of eternity, our mind just boggles. We cannot get our arms around that idea at all. All we really know is this earthly incarnation, and here time is marked very clearly for us every day. We carefully measure out each day in minutes and hours. We measure out a year in weeks and months and seasons. When we think about the span of a human lifetime, time seems heavily marked. If someone were to be lucky enough to live to be ninety, we would say that it was a good, long life. But ninety years is nothing in the larger scheme of things. Nothing. After this life comes our eternal life. And yet, the idea of eternity baffles us. "Eternity" is not an easy concept, and sometimes we feel overwhelmed. That response is perfectly understandable. But the truth is—the existence of an eternity is the only thing that makes any sense.

Pope John Paul II, in the course of his pontificate of 27 years, made many friends the world over among Catholics and non-Catholics alike. Many people have said that being in his presence brought them an almost indescribable, but overwhelming feeling of peace. He described faith as "an act of trusting abandonment to Christ." Trusting abandonment. What an interesting combination of words. At first, it seems like an oxymoron. Trust is the opposite of abandonment, at least in the common vernacular. And yet, Pope John Paul makes this combination work. In effect, we are asked to abandon, or surrender, ourselves to our heavenly Father's loving trust. I once heard my local priest, a wonderful man, say this about faith: "Just do the best you can and give it to God, and let Him do the rest." How many times have you heard some version of that idea from your parents? How many times have you said the same thing to your children? Just do the best you can. That is all we can ask. We are right back to our earlier image of the loving father standing on the shore, watching his son being hammered by the ocean. While you are floundering in the waves, just say, "Heavenly Father, I am doing the best I can. I give my best effort to you, and I know that you will make it worthwhile."

So, let us go back to Hamlet and what he has to say to us. Hamlet is a thinking man, a scholar, and he resents the feeling that he has surrendered control of his own life. He loves his father very much, and thinks him to be the finest man that he has ever known. But when his father's spirit comes back from the afterlife and demands that Hamlet avenge his murder, Hamlet feels annoyed, at some deeply personal and almost visceral level. He refers to his life as a "machine," or a tool in someone else's hands. Although he loves his father, he resents this intrusion, as is clearly shown from his closing lines in act one: "The time is out of joint. O cursed spite/ That ever I was born to set it right." He must put all his personal hopes and dreams on a shelf and address this demand from his dead father. He is not even sure that what he has been asked to do is ethical.

He has clearly shown himself to be a moral man, earlier in the play. When we see him in Act I, scene 2, after he witnesses his mother having proclaimed Claudius her new husband and his king, he is angry and resentful. He feels like his mother has shown the greatest disrespect for his dead father by marrying his father's brother so soon after the late King Hamlet's death. Right now, he believes, as does everybody else in Denmark, that his father died of a massive heart attack, perhaps brought on by the sting of a venomous serpent, because a toxin was present in his father's blood. Little does he know that the "serpent that did sting his father's life now wears his crown." Still, he believes that his mother, by marrying so quickly after her husband's passing, has shown the greatest disrespect to his father, and also to him. After all, he is a grown man, thirty years old, and he should have inherited the crown at the moment of his father's passing. However, by marrying Claudius, and proclaiming him king, she makes Hamlet wait to come into his inheritance. Probably he feels like her actions call into question his ability to be king. No matter what, he is angry and hurt. He even considers the possibility of suicide. But he decides against it, saying that he knows that God forbids that action:

O, that this too too solid flesh would melt,

Thaw, and resolve itself into a dew!

Or that the Everlasting had not fixed

His canon 'gainst self-slaughter. O God! God!

How weary, stale, flat, and unprofitable

Seem all the uses of this world!

Fie on it! Fie! Tis an unweeded garden

That grows to seed; things rank and gross in nature

Possess it merely.

Poor Hamlet! Talk about a dark hour of the soul.

He feels embarrassed to be left empty handed, when

he thought he was about to inherit his father's

crown. He feels bewildered by his mother's

actions, which seem to him to border on infidelity.

He wonders if she ever really loved his father as he

thought she did. He sees his uncle as a cheap

opportunist, but he has apparently wrested the crown from his grasp and has been accepted by the Danish people. His heart is full of despair, but he will not take his life because the Everlasting has forbidden that.

So, throughout the play, we see that Hamlet is a deeply spiritual character, but he is torn and nearly overwhelmed by the situation in which he finds himself. Three scenes later, he meets with his father's spirit, and the late King Hamlet tells his son that Claudius murdered him in his garden while he slept, pouring a deadly poison in his ear that curdled his blood and made him die of a heart attack. Claudius, his own brother whom he loved and trusted, sent him to his personal day of judgment without a chance to prepare his soul for passage, and then stole his wife and his crown. He asks Hamlet to avenge this murder, telling him that the "royal bed of Denmark" should not be a couch for lust, murder, and incest. At the moment, Hamlet quickly accepts this duty from his father, but he soon afterwards has second thoughts, wondering if this is action that he is about to undertake, killing the new king of Denmark, is a sin or an ethical and necessary action.

By the end of the play, he has decided that he must do this thing, and he wants the whole story to be told, and the people of Denmark to know why he proceeded as he did. He has proof of what he says, and he entrusts it to his dear friend Horatio, who will be his voice and who will tell his story after he dies. In the last scene of the play, he walks into a duel against Laertes (a duel that Claudius has set up) suspecting in his heart that it is some kind of a trap. Although Horatio tries to talk him out of participating in the duel, Hamlet says that he must see this thing through. If he dies, he dies, but he is

not going down without taking Claudius with him.

After all, he says, death is inevitable, and if this is

his moment, then he is as spiritually ready as he

could ever be. We end up with this famous passage

from Hamlet, right before he walks into the ill-fated

duel:

There's a special providence in the fall of a

sparrow. If it be now,

'tis not to come; if it be not to come, it will be now;

if it be not now, yet

it will come; the readiness is all. Since no man has

aught of what he

leaves, what is it to leave betimes. Let be(5.2.30-

235).

On a first reading, this passage can seem

bewildering, and even sound just a little bit like

eloquent double talk. But it is anything but that.

Let us begin with that first line. What is

Hamlet talking about? The lines are built on an

allusion to a famous passage from Matthew:

Nothing is covered that will not be revealed, or

hidden that will not be

known. What I tell you in the dark, utter it in the

light, and what you

hear whispered, proclaim upon the housetops...Are

not two sparrows

sold for a penny? And not one of them will fall to

the ground without

your Father's will. But even the hairs on your head

are all numbered.

Fear not, therefore; you are of more value than

many sparrows

(Matthew 10:26-33).

First off, that first image would be a great comfort

to Hamlet, because he wants the truth revealed. His

uncle Claudius killed the late King Hamlet in a

secret, vicious murder, and stole the throne. He is

clearly willing to kill Hamlet too in order to keep

his secret. Secondly, the image of the sparrow is

important. If our heavenly Father even knows

when a sparrow falls, then we can be sure that he

knows when our moment comes. He has even

counted all the hairs on our heads. We are that

precious to him. We are, each of us, worth more

than many sparrows. So, Hamlet comes to believe

that if this is the moment of his death, he will die

with peace and honor, having avenged his father's

death, proclaiming the truth to the people of Denmark, and passing the reign to a young man that he has watched from afar all his life and whom he believes will heal his country.

The final sentence in this famous passage essentially says that we leave all of our material possessions behind when we die. They are naught, in the final analysis. So, if this is so, what do they matter? They don't. Honor matters, and so does doing the right thing. Love matters.

The play *Hamlet* has a lot to say to us that is still very helpful and very relevant in our own time. Shakespeare suggests that when your honor is on the line, you have got to stand up for yourself, or you will feel like you have lost your soul already. He cautions us to understand that we must not fly off the handle too readily, but when your honor is on the line, that's different. As Hamlet says:

Rightly to be great is not to stir without great

argument,

But greatly to find quarrel in a straw,

When honor's at the stake(4.4.56-59).

Another important idea is the one that our heavenly

father is watching us from afar, and he knows the

secrets of our hearts. When our moment of passing

from this life to the next is upon us, he will attend

that passing. It will not go unnoticed. We will

come back to this idea later, when we meet Walt

Whitman. So, the play Hamlet helps us to see,

'through a glass darkly,' some very important ideas

about our time here on earth and how we should and

should not conduct ourselves. The character of

Hamlet is, in many ways, someone who can

reassure us that no man is perfect, and neither are

we. In spite of the fact that he is very smart and tries to live a moral life, he makes huge mistakes in the course of the story. On many occasions, he behaves very badly. He is mean-spirited and rude, he indulges in self-pity and whining, and he procrastinates. Pretty clearly, he feels overwhelmed by what he feels he must do. Still, when all is said and done, he behaves nobly, and he tries to do the right thing as best he understands it. That is what matters. And that is all any of us can do.

Another Mirror—the Dark Hour of the Soul—Ecclesiastes and Fitzgerald

In an "autobiographical novel" called *The Crack Up,* F. Scott Fitzgerald coins a term that has really come to speak to a lot of people in a very profound way. He said, "In the dark hour of the soul, it is always three o'clock in the morning." What he means is that, when you are on the edge of despair, the whole world seems to be blissfully asleep, except for you. And there you lie, with your eyes wide open, feeling completely alone, abandoned, and tormented by thoughts and regrets that won't leave you alone.

Everybody has some of those experiences sometime in their life—times when it just all overwhelms you. What you thought you had figured out about life seems to be all wrong, and nothing seems to make sense anymore. You find

yourself drifting, uncertainly, not sure what to

believe in. You feel as if the whole fabric of the

universe, as you know it, been ripped apart. That is

the dark hour of the soul.

When that happens, the big thing is to slow

down. To not make any decisions. Wait for the

morning. Things often look different in the

morning. In the middle of the night, that might not

seem like it could possibly be true. The darkness

can be overwhelming, but you just have to hang on.

The morning always comes. You get up, get in the

shower, wash your face and your hair, and get

dressed. Then, look outside again. Everywhere you

look, the day is beginning. People are getting ready

to face the day, and even if it feels like the world

has just ended for you, the very simple fact that

other people are getting up and moving toward the

business of the day is somehow reassuring. You feel empty—you feel like it is all nonsense. But, when this feeling overwhelms you, just keep putting one foot in front of the other. Go through the motions. Go through the motions.

There is a very interesting and peculiar book in the Old Testament, written about 350 B.C. It is called *Ecclesiastes,* and it is written by some unknown scholar who simply calls himself Qoheleth. That really just means "teacher". Many people have attributed authorship of the book to the wise King Solomon, but there is no real certainty about who the great philosopher of the text really is. Certainly, we are hearing the words of a brilliant man, and one who wrestled with many of the same questions that we are still battling with today. In the course of the book, he is pondering life, and the meaning of life, and he finds that the answers are beyond him. He says, when pulling his observations together: "When I applied my heart to know wisdom and to observe what is done on earth, I recognized that man is unable to find out all God's work that is done under the sun. However much man toils in searching, he does not find it out"(Ecclesiastes 8:16-17). He further says that whenever our hands find work to be done, we ought to just do it. Just do the best we can, keep putting one foot in front of the other, and trust. Recently, I have been thinking long and hard about four related words. "Thy will be done." I say those words every day when I pray, without really thinking about what they mean. And when you think about them, they can be really frustrating words, because it seems like we are powerless in the face of God's will. His will most certainly will be done, and there is nothing we can do about that. That can be a very frustrating idea. Until you think about it a little longer. We come back to Pope John Paul II's idea of "trusting abandonment." If you really think about it, in some strange way, these can be liberating words rather than frustrating ones. These words ask for a leap of faith—a trust that He loves us and wants us to be with him in heaven. But, if you can get your mind around the idea, "thy will be done," then you can relax and get about the business of doing the best you can with each day that is presented to you. Take care of the little things, and the big things will take care of themselves. Keep your focus small enough so that you don't get overwhelmed with it all.

The dark hour of the soul can come to any one of us. Sometimes, we are just exhausted, overwhelmed with what we have to do. Sometimes, there isn't enough money to make ends meet, and that can be frightening, especially if you have people who are relying on you to pay the bills. It is important to keep going. Don't look back and start to second-guess yourself. My wonderful friend, Father Tony Mulderry, says that there are three words that you have to drop out of your vocabulary when despair is threatening you. They are the following: "coulda," "woulda," and "shoulda." Perhaps you have made a mistake. Do the best you can to make it right, and then let it go. Put it in a box with the rest of emotional trash you are carrying around and take it to the dump. If you don't, it can paralyze you.

So, once again—keep your focus small and keep going. Keep working. If you feel yourself looking inward too much or too deeply, look outward. Everywhere around you are people who are secretly hurting, putting on a brave face, and doing the best they can. Join the parade. Look for the next thing to do, and do it with a willing heart. Ask your heavenly Father to send you some strength, and just fake it for a while. Doing can become being. Get back into the mix, into life, and you will slowly feel your burdens grow a little bit lighter. Fitzgerald had it right, and he knew a little bit about the dark hour of the soul from intense, personal experience. In fact, his self-made demons conquered him, and he was dead by the age of 44, having essentially destroyed himself and all his genius through alcoholism. Sadly, his life is like a cautionary tale for all of us. In the deep of night, when you lie awake, and it seems as if the whole of the world is asleep, the dark hour of the soul can overwhelm you. Fitzgerald also writes about this idea in his novel entitled *The Great Gatsby.* When Gatsby finally realizes that Daisy doesn't love him, and isn't coming back to him, he is broken and lost.

He wanders out to his pool, and the summer is over.

There is coolness in the air, and Gatsby has lost his

drive to live, having given up on his quest for his

holy grail—Daisy, the woman with the voice that

has the sound of money. He has waited for her

telephone call, and by now, he probably knows that

she isn't going to call. In fact, she was never going

to call, having retreated behind the screen of her

earthly wealth:

If that was true he must have felt that he had lost the

old warm

world, paid a high price for living too long with a

single dream.

He must have looked up at an unfamiliar sky

through frightening

leaves and shivered as he found what a grotesque

thing a rose is

and how raw the sunlight was upon the scarcely

created grass.

A new world, material without being real, where

poor ghosts,

breathing dreams like air, drifted fortuitously

about…like that

ashen, fantastic figure gliding toward him through

the amorphous trees.

Fitzgerald asks us to imagine Gatsby floating

listlessly in the pool, having lost the "old dream,"

and never seeing the man who has come, slipping

like a wraith, through the trees to take his life.

Wilson kills him, supposedly in revenge for Gatsby

killing his wife, a crime that Gatsby had not

committed. Daisy had done that. Stupid,

mercenary, disappointing, fickle Daisy. Like Nick

Carraway says, Gatsby was worth more than the

whole lot of them. But having lost his dream, he

has, at this point in the novel, lost his will to live.

The dark hour of the soul came in the form of a

silent telephone. It has an infinite number of forms.

However, the end of the novel picks up from

this moment and gives us another perspective. Nick

Carraway, the narrator of the novel, is thinking back

over the events of the past year, and the

senselessness of Gatsby's death, the arrogant

cruelty of the reckless people of the world—like

Tom and Daisy, and his own loss of innocence.

Still, rather than let the dark hour of the soul

overwhelm him, we hear some interesting and

enigmatic words. Delivered in its famously brilliant

elegiac tone, Nick closes the novel with this insight:

"Gatsby believed in the green light, the orgiastic

future that year by year recedes before us. It eluded us then, but that's no matter—tomorrow we will run faster, stretch out our arms farther...and one fine morning—So we beat on, boats against the current, borne back ceaselessly into the past"(159).

There has been much speculation about the meaning of that last line, and most critics see it as pessimistic. Essentially, they say that Fitzgerald is saying that we are trapped by our pasts. The current of our pasts draws us backwards, even as we struggle to row forward to the green light. Many critics say that the line can be interpreted on a personal level for Gatsby or for any one of us, and on a larger level for the United States of America herself. In both instances, they argue, the interpretation should be a pessimistic one. Notice that, in this set of lines from Fitzgerald, he sees us as continuing to struggle bravely, running faster and stretching our arms out farther. That sentence ends

with a thought left unfinished, "and one fine

morning—". The words just hang there,

incomplete, perhaps suggesting the folly of our

pursuit, of our even daring to dream. All of that

seems like a legitimate interpretation, one that is

borne out by the text. However, isn't it at least

possible to see the lines in a completely different

way?

Fitzgerald says that "Gatsby believed in the

green light," and he goes on to define the green

light as the "orgiastic future that year by year

recedes before us." That definitely does sound

pessimistic, suggesting the idea that the more we

pursue our dreams and our goals, and the longer we

live, we only discover that we will never get there.

Furthermore, like Gatsby, we may come to know

that even our most fervent dreams were unworthy of

our mad pursuit. However, it is possible to read the lines in a more hopeful way. Gatsby believed in the green light: Gatsby believed in his heavenly Father. You could make the argument that Gatsby was true to his love for Daisy, even if she did not return his devotion. If she is his "holy grail," then he was true to his quest. He paid with his very life. What if the line about being borne back ceaselessly into our past is really a reference to heaven? Where were we before this earthly incarnation? We cannot answer that question right now, although we desperately would like to do so. Still, the point is this. Most people admire the character of Gatsby, and we admire him because he was, in his own way, trying to do the best he could to love Daisy. Sure, his efforts are misdirected, clumsy, and ill-fated, and she is never worthy of his devotion.

Nonetheless, he kept the faith. That is worth something.

So, maybe what Fitzgerald is saying to us in this famous closing passage is that, in the final analysis, the struggle is the only thing that matters. So, when the dark hour of the soul threatens to overwhelm you, keep swimming or struggling, or—like Gatsby—running with your arms outstretched.

Another Study of Love—Shakespeare's
King Lear

God is love. Oh, I can almost hear you

saying…."God is love? I have heard those words a

million times, and I still don't know what they

mean. It doesn't even make sense to me. If God is

love, then why do so many bad things happen in the

world?" Good question.

And not so easy to answer. But, first of

all—we need a "definition of terms" clarification.

What is love? One of the best and most thorough

definitions comes from St. Paul's first letter to the

Corinthians, chapter 13, the opening passage of this

essay. There he writes: "Love is patient and kind;

love is not jealous or boastful; it is not arrogant or

rude. Love does not insist on its own way; it is not

irritable or resentful; it does not rejoice at wrong,

but rejoices in the right. Love bears all things, believes all things, hopes all things, endures all things. Love never ends." First of all, that is a pretty awesome challenge. People toss the word "love" around very casually these days. If we hold ourselves to St. Paul's definition of love, we will find that we must be quite a bit more careful with the word. Still, we are all capable of that awesome gift. And although we are hardly ever always true to St. Paul's high expectations, we are—almost all of us—frequently true to most of his definition. Notice that the act of loving is the act of giving. Love is not concerned with what is being repaid or answered. It is freely given. In fact, it gives and gives and gives—both energy and spiritual strength. Parents know this feeling about their children. From the moment your babies came into the world, you would do anything to protect them. I know that is true for me and for my husband. Anything. Their lives are our responsibility. However, that does not mean satisfying their every whim the moment they cry out for something. Even if we could have done that, we would not have acted in this way. What kind of parents would we be? What kind of child would we have been raising? It is not that simple. Still, we would do everything in our power to keep them safe, help them learn about their world, and know that they are profoundly loved.

And if we know this, human and deeply flawed as we are, how much more does our heavenly Father know this. It cannot even be imagined. But, here's an interesting thought—if God is love, then we know a little bit about God through our loving. Whenever we love someone— put their needs above our own, hold our tongue, support and care, hopefully endure, and keep the faith—we are more like God. When we love, we approach God. Our faith tells us that He is in us. How many times did Jesus himself try to get that idea across to the Apostles? He tells his disciples, and he speaks to us too: "Whatever you do to the least of my children, you do to me." He also tells us over and over that his Father loves us—loves us beyond our understanding. You remember these words from Matthew that we spoke about earlier: "Are not two sparrows sold for a penny? And yet not one of them will fall to the ground without your Father's will. But even the hairs of your head are all numbered. Fear not, therefore; you are of more value than many sparrows." We can make our life mission a lot simpler if we look with the eyes of faith. That word—faith—is a stumbling block for a lot of people. They say, I just can't surrender. I just can't say that I believe. I have more doubt than faith.

That is a very honest and a very legitimate answer. I once heard a priest say that we ought to embrace our doubts, because a faith that has no doubts is not a living faith. If we are searching, we are not lost. If we are questioning, we have not given up on an answer. So, if you cannot say about yourself, "I will look with the eyes of faith," then say, "I will look with the eyes of love." Love the ones that are entrusted to you. Use St. Paul's lofty definition, and trust that your heavenly Father appreciates the effort. It is just that simple, and just that difficult.

One of the most powerful definitions of love in the Shakespearean canon comes to us from the play entitled *King Lear*. Lear is the protagonist of the play, and he is an old man who knows nothing about love. When the play opens, Lear—who is at

least 80 years old—announces that he has decided

to abdicate power. He has three daughters and no

sons, so he says he is going to hold a public contest

to see which of his three daughters loves him the

most. He has divided the kingdom into three

unequal parts, and he says he will give the richest

third to the one who loves the most. What he really

means, however, is the one who speaks the prettiest

words of love. He fully intends to give the richest

third to the youngest daughter, Cordelia, who is

clearly the only daughter who loves him. However,

the first two girls, even though they despise him, are

very willing to play his stupid game. The first-born

daughter, Goneril, says that she loves him more

than sun and moon and stars, deeper than the ocean,

wider than the sky. The second daughter, Regan,

essentially just says that he can double what Goneril

has said. Pleased with their phony proclamations, he puffs up like a peacock, waiting for what Cordelia will say. She will not play the game. When he warns her that if she will not, she will ruin her fortune, she answers simply: "Unhappy that I am, I cannot heave / My heart into my mouth. I love your Majesty / According to my bond; no more nor less"(1.1.93-95). When he threatens her with exile, she tries to make him realize that the other girls are lying to him, but once his rage is kindled, it spins out of control. He banishes her on pain of death, saying it would be better if she had never been born, and he banishes the one honest advisor that tries to speak on her behalf. He surrenders himself to his two evil daughters who quickly strip him of his power and send him out into a storm, penniless and old.

There he learns. In the midst of his great suffering, he starts to lose him mind. However, in the brilliant paradox that is at the heart of this play—as he loses him mind, he begins to gain in wisdom. Stripped of the false sense of security that earthly wealth can give a man, he learns three important lessons. First and foremost, he learns what love is and what it is not. It has nothing to do with pretty words, titles, wealth, and parcels of land. It has everything to do with putting another person's needs ahead of your own. As he stands out there in the rain and cold, his court jester begs him to seek shelter, but at the same time, refuses to leave Lear's side. At the pivotal moment of the play, Lear decides to seek the fragile protection of a cave out on the heath, not for himself, but for his fool's sake. It might be the first time in his whole life that Lear has put the needs of someone else ahead of his own.

It is the beginning of an understanding of what love
is, and therefore, it is the beginning of wisdom:

My wits begin to turn.
Come on, my boy. How dost, my boy? Art cold?
I am cold myself. Where is this straw, my fellow?
The art of our necessities is strange
And can make vile things precious. Come, your
hovel.
Poor Fool and knave, I have one part in my heart
That's sorry yet for thee(3.2.68-73).

It's interesting that the speech begins with the
words "My wits begin to turn." By that, Lear
means that he feels that he is losing his grip on
sanity. However, the paradox is that even as he is
losing his mind, he gains in wisdom. If he is
descending into madness, it is a divine madness.

He immediately understands that his Fool will not leave his side, and that he is suffering. He agrees to go with Kent and the Fool to the shelter, but only for the Fool's sake. Still, this is an important moment because it is the first time he has had an understanding of love. Love means that you will put someone else's needs ahead of your own. As St. Paul says, "Love is patient and kind…Love does not insist on its own way; it is not irritable or resentful." This kind of love is the very love that Lear learns about in the midst of his suffering. His evil daughters say that their father must learn his lessons the hard way, and maybe they were right. But he learns. As he stands out their in the cold, he learns. He realizes that he has never been a good king and that he has never taken care of the poor of his country. He experiences the suffering that the homeless know every night of their lives and he

136

realizes that he has been deaf and dumb to their plight:

Poor naked wretches, whereso'er you are,

That bide the pelting of this pitiless storm,

How shall your houseless heads and unfed sides,

Your looped and windowed raggedness, defend you

From seasons such as these? Take physic, pomp;

Expose thyself to feel what wretches feel,

That thou mayst shake the superflux to them,

And show the heavens more just(3.4.28-36).

By "looped and windowed raggedness," he means that the poor wear ragged clothing that cannot keep them warm. When he says, "Take physic, pomp," he means essentially, "Learn a lesson, wealthy man." He then goes on to say that the wealthy of the world should experience biting poverty, and then they would know that they should shake their "superflux," or bounty, down to those less fortunate, thereby making the earthly world more just.

Justice is another important idea that Lear learns about. As his madness deepens, although, as we said, it may be more appropriate to call it a 'divine madness,' since Lear acquires a kind of heavenly wisdom that has eluded him when he was 'sane,' he learns that what our world calls justice is often not justice at all. He makes his way to Dover Beach, and there he surrenders to visions that torment him. As the storm continues to rage, he seems to think that perhaps Judgment Day has come at last. As he imagines sinners lining up for judgment, he realizes that earthly justice is frequently not just. The poor pay for everything; the rich get away with murder:

Through tattered clothes great vices to appear;

Robes and furred gowns hid all. Plate sin with gold,

And the strong lance of justice hurtless breaks;

Arm it in rags, a pigmy's straw does pierce

it(4.6.168-171).

Too often we have seen the bitter truth of this

cynical statement. Lear says, in this same scene

that we cry when we are born, and we will leave

this "great stage of fools" crying once again.

However, through the hard work of loyal

friends and servants, he is reunited with his lovely

daughter Cordelia before he dies. Although the

play ends with both of them dying, Lear gets to

stand proudly in her arms, protecting her from

harm, or so he thinks. As he does so, he speaks to

her, and we can see that he has learned what love is.

To be happy is to be in the presence of the one you

love, to keep them safe, and to just have time together. Love has nothing to do with power or wealth. Love is itself the only treasure worth having. As St. Paul says, "There where your treasure is, there also will your heart be." Lear clearly understands that. He stands with his arm around Cordelia, as they are about to be led away to prison, and—for this brief moment—he is absolutely clear about what matters and what doesn't:

Come, let's away to prison;
We two alone will sing like birds in the cage.
When thou dost ask me blessing, I'll kneel down
And ask of thee forgiveness. So, we'll live,
And pray, and sing, and tell old tales, and laugh
At gilded butterflies, and hear poor rogues
Talk of court news; who's in, who's out,

And take upon us the mystery of things

As if we were God's spies(5.3.8-17).

Notice that this man, who was so proud and so angry that he could not even hear Cordelia explain why she refused to play his silly game now knows that none of that matters at all. He will count himself a happy man, even if he is in prison, if he can just pass the time of day with her. Love comes in the seemingly unimportant moments of life, of just being together. The good news here is that we can know the experience of the most profound love every day. We just have to open our hearts and our minds to it. And when we love, we can be "God's spies" in the kingdom of earth. We can be his eyes and ears.

And Now—the Sacred Hurt and

Hemingway

Ernest Hemingway grew up in Illinois and summered in Michigan. When he was a young man, he first worked as a journalist, but when WWI started, he went over to Europe and volunteered as an ambulance driver for the Italian army. He was only nineteen years old. In the war, he saw things that he could never have imagined. He probably went in believing that war was the ultimate test of a man's courage. I am very certain that this idea underwent some qualifications and redefinitions pretty quickly as he experienced the reality of war. No matter what, he came through the whole experience with a vision—a vision that he went on to perfect in his later writings. In his vision, life is a battlefield, in which everyone is eventually wounded—either physically or spiritually. Defeat is inevitable—every one of us will die. Given this set of assumptions, it is important to play the game well. It is important to do the right thing, even if no one is looking. A man should strive to have grace under pressure, to achieve that quiet, inner grace whereby he knows who he is and what he believes in, and he acts accordingly. Bad things and unfair things will continue to happen to him in the course of his life, but he will soldier on bravely and he will conduct himself with dignity. Oddly enough, that is not too different from what St. Paul says in his Second Letter to Timothy. This letter comes at the end of St. Paul's wonderful career, and he knows that his time on earth is coming to an end. He writes: "I have fought the good fight, I have finished the race, I have kept the faith."

Ernest Hemingway's first novel is *The Sun Also Rises*. He was only about twenty six years old when he wrote it. Maybe he got the idea for the wound he gave his main character from some of the young men he had seen wounded in the war. Remember the allegory? Life is a battlefield and everyone is eventually wounded, either physically or spiritually. In this novel, the protagonist is a young man named Jake Barnes. He is 34 years old, and to an untrained eye, he looks whole. He looks like he has come through the war unscathed. But nothing could be further from the truth. Jake Barnes can no longer make love to a woman. And he has found the woman he loves. Just stop for a minute and really try to imagine that.

Although the lady says she loves Jake, she will not marry him because she says that she know that she would cheat on him and that would hurt him terribly. In the early parts of the novel, Jake begs her to reconsider, saying that he would be able to survive her infidelities. She says that she knows it will not work. At this point, Jake has clearly not learned how to soldier on bravely. On several different occasions, he begs her to love him. At night, the "dark hour of the soul" overwhelms him and he cries. The interesting thing is that to most people, Jake looks like he has got it all. He has money, a good job, and handsome friends. He is living in Paris, working for a newspaper, and he has Lady Brett Ashley. But of course, he does not have her at all. He can only hunger for her.

Of all the crazy things, Hemingway went to the Old Testament for the inspiration for this novel...for the inspiration and for the title. You remember, the book Ecclesiastes was written about 350 B.C. by a man who called himself Qoheleth, which simply means "teacher." This very unique book is more a collection of the reflections of a philosopher than a statement of belief. The author seeks to understand, by use of reason, the meaning of human existence and the good which man can find in life. He decides that "all is vanity," a breath, unsubstantial and fleeting. He further decides that God is inscrutable, and that the meaning of life is beyond our powers of reasoning, as we know them now. Still, the conclusion that he reaches is that we must face facts, accept what cannot be changed, and enjoy whatever good things God permits us during this life.

The title of Hemingway's novel actually comes from some of the opening lines:
"The sun goes down, and the sun also rises. It hastens to the place where is rises. The wind blows to the south and goes round to the north; round and

round goes the wind, and on its circuits the wind returns. All streams run to the sea, but the sea is not full…What has been is what will be and what has been done is what will be done; and there is nothing new under the sun. Is there a thing of which it is said, 'See, this is new?' It has been already in the ages before us." These are puzzling and mysterious lines, and yet we cannot help feeling that there is some important truth here.

But, we have to work for it. And it is easy to miss it, because the words are so simple, it almost seems like we are hearing double talk, or that which is obvious. What does all of this mean—the sun sets and rises…the wind blows around and around, the water runs to the sea? We feel ourselves saying, all right…I will grant you that…but so what? What does it all mean? We have to slow our engines down and think—kind of feel our way into the wisdom. Gently.

What Qoheleth seems to be saying is that there is a pattern, a plan, and we cannot understand all of it. The sun seems to rise in the morning (we know from science of course that this is not what is really happening) and it seems to set in the evening. For our purposes, we will say that the sun rises and sets every day. There is a plan, and there is a time. The wisdom goes way beyond the sun and a day. Metaphorically, what the writer is saying, of course, is that we are born, we live our life—our appointed time, and then we die. We cannot know for sure what is beyond this life, but many of the most brilliant people that have ever breathed have fought their way through many questions and arrived at the leap of faith of which Jesus spoke to us. There is a heavenly Father watching over his creation, and we are an important part of that creation. In the great poem entitled "Song of Myself" by Walt Whitman, he talks about his belief, something that he arrived at almost reluctantly, that every single thing that had ever happened conspired together to give birth to him. All of creation was urging itself toward the moment when he would be brought into the world. Each of us can say the same thing. And it is true.

So, the patterns of the universe—of our heavenly Father's creation—are appointed and monitored. God has appointed that the sun will rise and will set, in an orderly fashion—that the winds will move around the earth, and that the rivers will flow to the sea. The cycles and circles of life go on, and for our moment, we step into the celestial dance. Now, back to Hemingway. During our time on the dance floor, some wonderful things are going to happen to us, and some painful things are going to happen. That is true for everyone, and no one is exempted from experiencing pain and loss. Now, for existentialists like Qoheleth and Hemingway, the answer about how to handle this basic fact is not exactly anchored in the presence of a loving God. However, the answer that they arrive at brings them right back to the faith-based anchor that a person of faith might arrive at. We cannot know the mysteries of life--they are beyond the scope of our knowledge in this world, in this life. Still, we must live each day as well as we can, conduct ourselves with honor, do the right thing as best we can determine it, and soldier on bravely. We should enjoy the good things of life when they come our way, (drink our wine and eat our bread) accept what cannot be changed, cherish the experience of love, and move forward with dignity.

What an incredibly liberating philosophy that is. And it is really very simple to come to understand. However, it is not necessarily simple to put into practice. There are many temptations along the way, and our world frequently seems to tell us that we must get more, take more, keep more for ourselves. Truthfully, that is not the path to joy. There are no answers there, or perhaps there are answers, but they are not helpful at all. In *The Sun Also Rises,* there is a minor character named Count Mippipopolous. He is an older man, perhaps in his seventies, who has survived many battles and wars and has the scars to prove it. He arrives in Paris and meets Jake and Lady Brett Ashley and spends several evenings in their company. He is the kind of character we call an exemplar in Hemingway; that is, someone who has faced death and danger, survived, and even though wounded or compromised physically or spiritually, conducts himself with that admirable kind of quiet dignity and grace. Jake and the Count have several wonderful discussions in the early part of the novel, and the careful reader can feel the Count gently teaching Jake, although he would never presume to do so.

The Count buys expensive champagne. He insists that Jake and Brett wait to drink it until it is cooled to the proper temperature. He reminds them that it should be taken slowly, tasted, and enjoyed. When Brett Ashley gulps her champagne, he gently scolds her, saying that she must not just drink to get drunk. She should slow down, taste the wine, and enjoy the company. This sounds very much like old Qoheleth from Ecclesiastes, who says, "Go and eat your bread and drink your wine with a merry heart, for God has already approved that you should do so." When Jake tells the Count that he should write a book about wines, the Count says that all he wants out of wines is to enjoy them. Well, if we substitute the word life for the word wines, we come to wisdom. "All I want out of life is to enjoy it." Now, it is easy to misunderstand this statement as some kind of hedonistic creed. But, if we are careful about the word "enjoy" we might be less likely to make that blunder. Enjoy means come to joy. Now the word "joy" is a very special word—it means a feeling of peace and well-being, a contented heart. That is not a feeling that is reached by satisfying sensual pleasures in some kind of over stimulated, artificial orgy of delights. Rather, it is a quiet kind of peace and acceptance. In other words, an experience of grace.

One of the nicest things that the Count does in the novel is recognize Jake as a fellow exemplar, even though he probably suspects that Jake is still working his way through some serious problems, which, of course, he is. The Count says that each man must "get to know the values." Notice that this is an individual thing. A man must live his life, a fully examined life, weighing good and bad and figuring out what is important to him. Then, he knows what matters, what he values, where he can bend, and where he must stand his ground. When he figures that out, even though bad things may occasionally happen to him, he will always get his balance. No one is exempt from hurt, but if a man has figured out what is important to him, he is more likely to be able to survive the moment and the loss with his dignity intact. After the Count says this, he acknowledges Jake as a fellow exemplar, asking him if he has found the same thing to be true in his own life. Jake humbly, and with some quiet pleasure, accepts this graceful recognition from the Count, even though Jake know that he is still trying to figure out how to deal with the problem of his impossible relationship with Brett. A careful reader of the novel suspects that the Count believes that Jake will work his way through the many real and difficult questions and arrive at the status of an exemplary man. A man must know his place. We are not gods—we are men. As Qoheleth would say, "I applied my mind to know wisdom and to know madness and folly. I perceived that this also is but a striving after wind." There are things we can know and can do, and there are things that are beyond the scope of our earthly powers. We must come to terms with that.

In chapter three of Ecclesiastes, Qoheleth writes several lines that are very well known. Almost everyone has heard them, or part of them,

and can even repeat the words, even if they don't
know what they are quoting:

For everything there is a season, and a time for
every matter under heaven:
A time to be born, and a time to die,
A time to plant, and a time to pluck up what is
planted;
A time to kill, and a time to heal;
A time to break down, and a time to build up;
A time to weep, and a time to laugh;
A time to mourn, and a time to dance;
A time to cast away stones, and a time to gather
stones together;
A time to embrace, and a time to refrain from
embracing;
A time to seek, and a time to lose;
A time to keep, and a time to cast away,

A time to rend, and a time to sew,

A time to keep silence, and a time to speak;

A time to love and a time to hate;

A time for war, and a time for peace.

Qoheleth goes on to say that each man must try to discern these proper times for himself, honestly and without self-deception. And then, he must act accordingly, remembering to observe the proper times and to be happy and enjoy himself when he gets the chance: "for it is God's gift to man that every one should eat and drink and take pleasure in all his toil. I know that whatever God does endures for ever; nothing can be added to it, nor anything taken away from it; God has made it so." So Hemingway and Qoheleth tell us just about the same thing. Bad things are going to happen; no one is exempt from pain and loss. That is part of the human condition. In *The Sun Also Rises*, Hemingway uses the term "hurt" for this loss. Once a person has been "hurt" things are never the same. Things that were once thought possible are now understood to be impossible. Our options have been somehow changed or limited. Recognizing the loss, and accepting the parts of it that cannot be changed, we go on. We hold our heads high, continue to live our lives with dignity, paying attention to the proper times for each thing, and soldier on bravely. There is a beautiful dignity and joy in this understanding. In fact, in doing so, we have the only kind of victory that is really possible to us in this life.

This world is ephemeral. We can go back to Ecclesiastes for a moment here. He opens his wonderful book with the words, "All is vanity." If we think that we can control what will happen to us in this world, we are fools. If we think we can

triumph and become like gods, we are worse than

fools. We cannot seek to know the future; we must

live in the present, knowing that each day is a gift.

Seeking to know the future has been a temptation

for humankind probably since the beginning of

time. And it always gets us in trouble. If you have

read the wonderful Harry Potter saga, you know

that the most brilliant people in that story have a

profound mistrust for the "art of divination." In

fact, Harry, Hermione, and Dumbledore seem to

regard it as dangerous nonsense. In the sixth book

of the series, *Harry Potter and the Half Blood*

Prince, there is an unforgettable scene between

Harry and Dumbledore. Harry is overwhelmed with

the thought that he is somehow "fated" to have to

kill the evil Lord Voldemort. Why me? Why me?

Why has this fate fallen to me? Dumbledore spends

sometime with Harry, trying to help him understand that there are many 'prophecies' that have been made, and most of them do not come true. The prophecy only gains strength and credibility when we know it. In fact, if we do not know the prophecy, it does not exist. Dumbledore is at some pains to help Harry understand this very difficult notion: "If Voldemort had never heard of the prophecy, would it have been fulfilled? Would it have meant anything? Of course not! Do you think every prophecy in the Hall of Prophecy has been fulfilled?...If Voldemort had never murdered your father, would he have imparted in you a furious desire for revenge? Of course not! If he had not forced your mother to die for you, would he have given you a magical protection he could not penetrate? Of course not, Harry! Don't you see? Voldemort himself created his worst enemy, just as tyrants everywhere do! Have you any idea how much tyrants fear the people they oppress? All of them realize that, one day, amongst their many victims, there is sure to be one who rises against them and strikes back. Voldemort is no different. Always he was on the lookout for the one who would challenge him. He heard the prophecy and leapt into action, with the result that he not only handpicked the man most likely to finish him, he handed him uniquely deadly weapons...By attempting to kill you, Voldemort himself singled out the remarkable person who sits here in front of me, and gave him the tools for the job!"

The point that J. K. Rowling is brilliantly making in her saga is an important one. We must not ask to know the future. That is the province of our God. We must learn to live in the present, doing the best we can with what we know at that moment. So, it is not surprising that Harry, Dumbledore, and Hermione regard the "art of divination" as dangerous nonsense. They are right. But perhaps the most famous warning against the dangers of seeking to know the future was written about 430 B.C.

A Warning Against Hubris—the Timeless Lessons of *Oedipus Rex*

The ancient Greek playwrights wrote plays based on the stories of Greek mythology. This was really a very liberating choice, because every adult who came to see the plays already knew the story. The audience was not there to find out what happens—they were there to watch how and why it happens. In our educational terminology that is in use today, we would say that the audience was engaged in higher level thinking skills. How and Why are much more difficult questions than What.

Well, probably the most famous play from the ancient Greek world, (in fact many scholars have called it the grandfather of all plays) is the story *Oedipus Rex*. The action of the story really begins long before the play opens. King Laius and

163

Queen Jocasta want to know if they are going to have a child. As king, Laius is very anxious for an heir. He sends to the infamous Oracle at Delphi, and the answer makes his blood run cold. Yes, he will have a son, and that son will kill his own father and marry his own mother. Patricide and incest. Two terrible sins...sins that cry out for punishment.

In time, Jocasta delivers a baby boy, and King Laius gives the newborn child to a trusted shepherd and tells him to take the baby outside the palace gates and kill the child. Presumably, they would then announce that the baby was stillborn, or something to that effect. This faithful servant takes the child from Jocasta, and under the cover of darkness, he leaves the walled city of Thebes. He takes the baby up into the wilderness, to Mount Cithaeron. There, something happens. We cannot be sure what changes his mind. Perhaps he is moved with pity for the child. Perhaps he is afraid of punishment from the gods for killing a helpless baby. But, the bottom line is, he cannot bring himself to kill the child. Instead, he pierces the baby's heels with an iron stake, supposedly to keep him from crawling away, and leaves the baby in the hands of the gods. Now, at this point, there are some uncertainties in the text. Either he abandoned the baby in this condition, or he gave the wounded baby to another shepherd...a shepherd from the town of Corinth, located on the other side of the mountain range. But he could not have expected what would happen after that.

This other shepherd took the baby, under the cover of darkness to the king and queen of Corinth, who were also childless. They embraced the baby as a gift from the gods, told everyone that Queen Merope had conceived and given birth to the child in secret and the child is their own flesh and blood. They raised him as their own son, and never told him of the strange circumstances of his birth. In time, there was a banquet, and Oedipus, now a young man, heard some drunk loudly proclaim that he was a bastard, and not his father's child. He fought back his embarrassment and confronted his parents the next day. They assured him vehemently that the drunk had lied and that he was in fact their own flesh and blood.

Oedipus seemed to be satisfied with what they had said, but he really was not. So, without consulting further with his parents, he set out for the Oracle at Delphi, determined to get some answers. He asked the Oracle, "Am I my father's son?" And the Oracle answered, "Yes. And you will kill your own father and marry your own mother." Hearing these terrible words, Oedipus decided, right then and there that he would never return home to

Corinth, fearing that he might commit these terrible

sins. Instead, he wandered, a man without a

country, in the wilderness world. We can assume

that his poor parents, Polybus and Merope, never

knew what had become of him.

In time, he came to a famous crossroads, a

place where three roads meet. He was alone, a

young man on horseback. Coming down another

road was an elderly man in a carriage, attended by

five or six servants. Oedipus believed he had the

right of way, and therefore refused to yield to this

old man and his retinue of servants. Perhaps they

had the right of way, and perhaps they just felt like

they should have it because they were royalty and

this young man was a nobody. We cannot know.

But we know what happened. The old man told his

servant to strike Oedipus and knock him from his

horse. Instead, Oedipus clobbered the servant.
Then, the old man took a goad, a nasty metal club,
and tried to strike Oedipus on the head with this.
Certainly, this could have been a fatal blow.
Instead, Oedipus caused the horses to rear, the
carriage to flip over, and he then killed every single
one of them he could, including the old man. One
servant managed the escape with his life, but
Oedipus, in his great rage, killed at least six men.
We know, even as we read about this event, that he
has now killed his own father. Oedipus will find
out in the full horror of time.

Then Oedipus journeys on to the city of
Thebes and finds a city in distress. Their king has
been murdered and a terrible beast, a Sphinx, has
taken up residence at the gates of the City. While
she is there, the city is suffering—the wells have
dried up, the babies are stillborn, the crops have

failed, and the lamentation of the suffering Thebans is a constant and hopeless wailing. Only when someone answers her riddle will the plague be lifted. Many young men try to answer it, and all are killed when they fail. The prize is worth the risk…the man who can answer the riddle will be given the hand of the lovely Queen Jocasta in marriage. The riddle is puzzling. What walks on four legs in the morning, two legs in the afternoon, and three legs in the evening?

Young Oedipus arrives at the city in the fullness of time. He has nothing to lose, and nowhere to go, so he decides to try his hand at the riddle. After the Sphinx poses her question, he thinks about it. He later tells us that he figured it out all by himself. He gives the correct answer…a man. A man crawls as an infant—in the morning of his life, walks erect as a man, and uses a cane in the evening of his days. The Sphinx flies away, screeching angrily, and the plague is lifted. The City of Thebes returns to health, and they proudly present Queen Jocasta to young Oedipus. They marry and she bears him four children—two girls and two boys. Now, he has married his own mother, and the terrible prophecy is fulfilled.

In time, another plague befalls the city of Thebes and they are told that they must solve the murder of King Laius or the suffering will not end. Oedipus says that he will search heaven and earth for the answer. This is actually where the action of the play Oedipus Rex begins. You can see how important it is that the people already know the story if the playwright assumes that they know everything I have just told you. At any rate, now the quest begins. Now a lot of people want to say that none of this is Oedipus' fault. None of it. He was actually trying to do a good thing, and with some perverted sense of malicious humor, the gods turned his intended good actions against him. Not so fast.

We can make the argument that the sin of hubris is the cause of this whole disaster. The ancient Greeks believed that hubris was the most deadly sin of all. Hubris is the sin or excessive pride. Self-righteous pride. Believing yourself to be more than a man—almost a god. Believing that you are more important than anyone else. Refusing to humble yourself before your gods. Believing that you know better. Combine that kind of pride with great rage, and you've got hubris. It is a deadly combination, and we see it almost every day in our own world.

How is Oedipus guilty of hubris? Well, you could say that his attitude about what is said at the banquet is the first example of it. He is hurt and

embarrassed by the drunk's accusation that he is not

of royal blood. He is so wounded that he refuses to

accept the statements of his parents, and determines

to go to the Oracle to find out the truth. This in and

of itself is a dangerous decision, because everybody

knows that oracles tend to speak in riddles. Perhaps

this is because they are speaking of things that are

outside the appointed province of man's

understanding. If you go to consult an oracle, you

are asking to know something that is beyond the

reach of what you are allowed to know. What will

happen in the future? That is not for us to know.

We come right back to the lessons of Harry Potter.

We should not ask to know what the prophecies say.

The minute that we hear it, we subconsciously

move heaven and earth to make the prophecies

come true. It cannot help but influence the way we act.

Even easier than this is the fact that Oedipus is guilty of hubris at the crossroads. He was insulted, and he overreacted. He not only punished the servant who attacked him—he killed six men in his great rage, only allowing one to escape. And we can be pretty certain that he would have killed him too if he had been able to. When Oedipus confesses to this sin at the crux of the play, he says that he paid the insulting servant back, more than was his due. That is certainly true. He escalated the fight to a frightening degree, surrendering to a blood lust of rage. Nevertheless, it is important to remember that Oedipus is not the only one guilty of hubris. Certainly, the first sin belongs to Laius and Jocasta. First of all, they sought the oracle, seeking to know if they would have a child. Secondly, when Jocasta

173

gives birth to the child, they decide to kill the boy. Clearly, in making that decision, they have decided that King Laius' life is more important than that of the baby. Did Jocasta weep when she handed over the child? Did she surrender him willingly? Did she try to talk her husband out of this decision? We can only wonder. Still, no matter what, they put the child in the hands of that shepherd with the express order that he should take the child into the wilderness and "do him in."

What kind of parent could ever do such a thing? Unfortunately, it still happens in our world, and it has happened many, many times in different cultures all around the world. However, when it happens, it is at least arguable that we are looking at an instance of hubris, the unforgivable sin.

At the very least, one of the lessons that comes out of this play is a warning against trying to know or control the future by any other means than hard work and faith. Believing that we can outsmart or deceive God is the ultimate folly. We come back to Pope John Paul's idea of "trusting abandonment." We must trust in the Lord, do the best we can, offer our best to Him, and know that He will make our efforts worthy. Without Him, we can do nothing. With Him, all things are possible.

Twelfth Night—the Spunky Heroine Viola

A very good example of that kind of trusting abandonment comes to us from William Shakespeare's play entitled *Twelfth Night*. Shakespeare gives this festive comedy a subtitle, calling the play, in addition to its more famous title, *What You Will*. By that he means to suggest that we wish things worked out the way they do in this lovely little play. Most people know Shakespeare for his tragedies, and they are probably much more profound and thought provoking than the comedies. However, *Twelfth Night* is a wonderfully wise and gently philosophical play, with several important ideas for us to think about. The play is often dated at about 1600, although there is some dispute as to the exact time Shakespeare wrote it. Nonetheless, it is an excellent example of his work during his years of mastery. He knows exactly what he is doing. He is confident enough in his form and subject that he feels daring enough to experiment. What we have then, is a work of genius.

The heroine of the play is Viola, who is shipwrecked right before the play opens, landing penniless in a strange town called Illyria. She believes that her twin brother Sebastian has perished in the storm, although happily, she will be reunited with him, alive and well, by the end of the play. In many ways, this play is about second chances, about redemption. Still, as the play opens, Viola finds herself cast ashore in foreign territory, with no one to rely on but herself. She thanks the sea captain who has rescued her, borrows some men's clothing from him, and gets herself an introduction to Count Orsino's court, hoping to be employed as a pageboy. We can imagine her chopping her hair and binding her breasts, hoping to get this job. Her chances would be good, because she is literate, and there is a need for pageboys who can read and write. She takes on a new name with her disguise, calling herself Cesario. Not only does she get a job, within several days she has worked her way up the ladder to be the trusted envoy of Orsino to the Lady Olivia, whom he has been unsuccessfully courting for some time now. Orsino decides that there is something delicate and different about Cesario, and that she will succeed in winning Lady Olivia's heart for him. He thinks that maybe the other messengers he has sent have been too big and burly, and that this young man will have just the right touch. Little does he know how right he is, for the Lady Olivia, who has announced that she will not be seeing any men for a period of seven years, as she mourns her brother who has recently passed away, is immediately taken with this handsome and winsome young messenger—but not for Orsino. Rather, Olivia finds herself infatuated with the young pageboy. And to make things perfect, in the few days that Viola has worked for Orsino, she has fallen in love with him. So, young Viola finds herself in a very awkward love triangle, a mess totally of her own making. Yet, she does not despair or whine. Rather, she kind of decides to keep working and doing the best she can to fulfill her promise to Orsino, hoping that things will work out. In Act I, she surrenders to Time, saying that she knows she cannot control everything that will happen. When she discovers that Olivia has fallen for her, instead of her master, she feels a little overwhelmed. Still, we can hear that hopeful shrug of the shoulders, and her determination to keep on going, doing the best she can: "O Time, thou must untangle this, not I; / It is too hard a knot for me to untie"(2.2.40-41).

Olivia has been engaging is an extravagant show of mourning for her dead brother. Unlike Viola, who will find at the end of the play, that her brother is alive, no such "miracle" awaits Olivia. Her brother will not be coming back to life, as Sebastian seems to do for Viola. This too gives us an important insight. Shakespeare is no fool. He does not suggest that all losses can and will be redeemed by the end of a tragedy. That is just going too far. Shakespeare suggests that some losses cannot be undone. Sometimes our loved ones die, and we are heartbroken. That is part of the human condition. To pretend otherwise would just be folly. However, by the end of the play, Olivia will have fallen in love—finding a husband

and a sister-in-law, and she will get another lease on life because of this discovery. When these opportunities present themselves, both Olivia and Orsino are wise enough to embrace them readily, and in so doing, they show us how to live our lives.

The span of time that the play covers is three months, and for all of that time, Viola serves Orsino as faithfully as she can, trying desperately to win Olivia's heart for him, even though she is madly in love with him herself. In fact, there are several instances in the play where Viola tries to tell him how much she loves him. Of course, he thinks he is speaking to his pageboy, Cesario, whom he seems to regard as something like a younger brother, and so their dialogue is fraught with irony and understated sexual tension. In Act 2 scene 4, they are sitting together listening to some sad music that Orsino is having his musicians play. He looks at

Cesario's face, and asks if he has ever been in love. Viola replies that she was once in love with someone about his age, coloring, and complexion. Orsino blusters, telling Cesario that a man should always love a woman younger than himself, because women's beauty tends to fade very quickly. Viola sits at his feet, hearing this, her poor heart breaking just a little bit more. However, it is very clear to us that Orsino doesn't have any idea what love is. Not a clue. He then tries to send Viola back to Olivia, where she does not want to go, knowing full well that Olivia has a crush on Cesario, who doesn't even really exist. She tells him that he may have to learn to accept no for an answer, that maybe Olivia just doesn't love him. She even suggests that perhaps there is a woman who loves him dearly, and if he doesn't love her, that's the end of it. You can't order someone to love you. He says that women are not capable of

that depth of passion. Then, she gently teaches him

about love:

Orsino: There is no woman's sides

Can bide the beating of so strong a passion

As love doth give my heart; no woman's heart

So big to hold so much. They lack retention…

Make no compare

Between that love a woman can bear me

And that I owe Olivia.

Viola: Ay, but I know…too well what love women

to men may owe.

In faith, they are as true of heart as we,

My father had a daughter loved a man

As it might be, perhaps, were I a woman,

I should your lordship.

Orsino: And what's her story?

Viola: A blank, my lord. She never told her love,

But let concealment, like a worm in the bud,

Feed on her damask cheek. She pined in thought…

She sat like Patience on a monument,

Smiling at grief. Was not this love indeed?

We men may say more, swear more, but indeed,

Our shows are more than will, for still we prove

Much in our vows, but little in our love(2.4.93-118).

She sits there quietly, spinning out this story about

her fictional "sister," when she is, of course,

speaking about her love for Orsino. As far as she

can tell, it is a hopeless love. He seems to be in

love with Olivia, or at least he thinks he is. Beyond

that, he seems to consider her something like a kid

brother, a young man whom he can help to mold

with his "wisdom" about love and women.

However, even in this moment when her heart is

184

breaking, she is teaching him about love. She is also getting him to consider the possibility that he underestimates women and their depth of feeling. At the end of the play, in the wonderful final scene, these things that she has said to him will come back to him, and then he will understand. He will realize that he had only seen "through a glass darkly," and now he will be ready to see more clearly.

One of the most endearing things about Viola is her good heart. She has a kind of quiet courage that guides her, and she looks to the future with hope. It all works out for her. In fact, in most of Shakespeare's comedies, things work out for the best for the characters that try to do the right thing. In his comedies, there is a kind of benevolent providence, tugging his characters toward a joyful conclusion, often in spite of themselves. Joy may not come in quite the way they thought it would, but it comes just the same. There is a gentle lesson for us there—wait and hope. Right now, we see only through a glass darkly, but someday we will see so much better. So, do the best you can with the moment you have, be honest with yourself about what is going on in your life, say thank you to those who have helped you on the journey, and look forward. With hope. Joy will quietly come and surprise you.

Made in the USA
Columbia, SC
26 December 2017